Things That Make Us Go; "Hmmm?"

Useless Information And Obscure Trivia

Chickie Toscano Woodburn

You recognize the song if you're a teenage product of the 1990s. "Things That Make You Go, 'Hmm?'" was a chart- topper for thirty- one weeks, according to wikipedia. If you don't recognize the title, then you can certainly find it on youtube.com if you wish to enjoy the song's comical lyrics. This piece, by C & C Music Factory, is one of many catchy works heard over the radio, for years, that 'stuck'. On the following pages you will learn, not only what those things are that make the singer ponder, 'hmm', but answers to many other questions we once thought of as rhetorical, but that actually do have a valid response. The answers to questions like, " What *did* Confucius say?", or, "When *is* it time to make the donuts?" are tackled with- in this fun and light collection.

Whether you want to show off your knowledge of random subjects at the next work- party or want to charm someone with your knowledge and wit, this book will be an amusing read and provide a plethora of what we might consider *Useless Information And Obscure Trivia* ©.

Table of Contents

Part One

Lyrical and Media References

What Are the Things That Make Us Go, "Hmm"?

The majority of Gen X and Y, and even a few baby boomers, will immediately reference this indelible song, 'Things That Make You Go, Hmm', by C+C Music Factory from 1991. The tune features Freedom Williams and a buxom vocalist named Martha Wash. C+C Music Factory had other hits from that same album, including 'Gonna Make You Sweat', that showcased the music video which drew the band into unseemly controversy. The group received bad press once it became public knowledge that they substituted Wash, the actual vocalist, with singer Zelma Davis. Davis, who lip- synced over Wash's track, appeared in the video simply because her look was considered more 'camera friendly', while Wash's full- figure was deemed less marketable. The scandal was widely broadcast in the news and attached itself to the C+C Music Factory name. In a 2014 article in Rolling Stones magazine, Jason Newman head- lined the disparagement, 'Martha Wash: The Most Famous Unknown Singer of the '90s Speaks Out', which provided the details just described. Surprisingly, 'Things That Make You Go, Hmm' has become a trendy term, despite the notoriety surrounding its history.

The vastly popular site, Pinterest, hosts multiple boards using the song name as their title. Memes and quotes reference it widely across the internet. There are a large number of compilations, (much like this tome), meant to prompt discussions around simple things, often overlooked, that should give us pause and make us think... ideas to make the reader ponder, *'Hmm?'.* Here is one tongue- in- cheek compilation to reflect on from one such tabulation, posted by *+jnelsoninjax* in a forum hosted by neowin.net. How many of these have you ever thought twice about?

"1. Why do we park in driveways and drive on parkways?

2. Do Lipton employees take coffee breaks?

3. Can I yell "movie" in a crowded firehouse?

4. Can you be a closet claustrophobic?

5. How do a fool and his money get together?

6. Why does Hawaii have interstate highways?

7. How is it that a building burns up as it burns down?

8. If a train station is where the train stops, what is a workstation?

9. If nothing ever sticks to Teflon, how do they make Teflon stick to the pan?

10. If the pen is mightier than the sword, and a picture is worth a thousand words, how dangerous is a fax?

11. If the police arrest a mime, do they tell him he has the right to remain silent?

12. What hair color do they put on the driver's licenses of bald men?

13. What was the best thing before sliced bread?

14. Why do banks charge you a "non-sufficient funds" fee on money they already know you don't have?

15. Why do they put Braille on the drive through bank machines?

16. If Barbie is so popular, why do you have to buy her friends?

17. If you get cheated by the Better Business Bureau, who do you complain to?

18. What are Preparation A through Preparation G?

19. In a country of free speech, why are there phone bills?

20. Did Washington flash a quarter when asked for ID?

21. How come there aren't B batteries?

22. If the post office has machines that can sort snail mail at 1000's of times per minute, then why do they give it to a little old man on a bike to deliver?

23. How do "Do not walk on the grass" signs get there?

24. Why do black olives come in cans and green olives come in jars?

25. Before they invented drawing boards, what did they go back to?

26. How is it possible to have a civil war?

27. If all the world is a stage, where is the audience sitting?

28. If love is blind, why is lingerie so popular?

29. If the #2 pencil is so popular, why is it still #2?

30. Why is the alphabet in that order? Is it because of that song?

31. If I melt dry ice, can I take a bath without getting wet?

32. Crime doesn't pay...does that mean that my job is a crime?

33. How do they get the deer to cross at that yellow road sign?

34. How do you know that honesty is the best policy until you have tried some of the others?

35. How do you throw away a garbage can?

36. How does a thermos know if the drink should be hot or cold?

37. How does the guy who drives the snowplow get to work in the mornings?

38. Do you realize how many holes there could be if people would just take the time to take the dirt out of them?

39. If a word in the dictionary were misspelled, how would we know?

40. If you're in a vehicle going the speed of light, what happens when you turn on the headlights?

41. What happens to an 18 hour bra after 18 hours?

42. Why didn't Noah swat those two mosquitoes?

43. Why do hot dogs come 10 to a package and hot dog buns only 8?

44. Why do tourists go to the tops of tall buildings and then put money into telescopes so they can see things on the ground close-up?

45. Why is it that bullets ricochet off of Superman's chest, but he ducks when the gun is thrown at him?

46. Why is it that night falls but day breaks?

47. Why is it that you must wait until night to call it a day?

48. What if the Hokey Pokey IS what its all about?

49. When your pet bird sees you reading the newspaper, does he wonder why you're just sitting there, staring at carpeting?

50. What happened to the first 6 'ups'?"

This is a pretty extensive list of ruminations. To be completely thorough, these are a few of the situations that gave Robert Clivillés and Freedom Williams reasons to pause according to the light- hearted, self-deprecating song lyrics to "Things That Make You Go, 'Hmm'?"; "Our hero gets seduced by a girl so his girlfriend can catch him cheating; his baby comes out looking like his best friend; and he finds out a girl who he thinks is *pure* has been 'Playing Tic Tac Toe,' which is a classic '90s saying for sleeping around." Those were the things that made these song- writers go 'Hmm...' I think anyone in their position would ponder the same!

...But I Won't Do That; What's THAT?!

Meat Loaf is a popular classic rock band of the seventies and eighties whose hit single from 1993 was entitled "I'd Do Anything for Love (But I Won't Do That)". It was a duet with female vocalist Lorrainne Crosby. In the chorus of the tune, singer Michael Lee Aday, nee Marvin Lee Aday, proclaims: *I would do anything for love, but I won't do that.* I'm among many who always believed that the remaining lyrics of the chorus failed to reveal exactly what "that" is, leaving even the most avid followers puzzled and wondering what *won't* this guy do for love? Apparently Meat Loaf's song- writer had anticipated this confusion among his audience, while Aday assured him that his fans would figure it out. We didn't. During a talk show featuring Aday for his celebrity as a singer and actor, the host pointedly inquired about the riddle of this tune. In this interview with Ali Wentworth, Aday revealed what "that" refers to:

"'It's the line before every chorus,' explained Loaf. 'There's nine of them, I think. The problem lies because Jimmy likes to write, so you forget what the line was before you get to 'I won't do that.' (Some of the things the song says he won't do: forget the way you feel right now; forgive himself if you don't go all the way tonight; do it better than he does it with you, so long; and stop dreaming of you every night of his life.)"

There you have it. Listen to the words at the end of each verse and just before the refrain for the answers. He makes it seem so obvious. There is one blatant exchange, however, as the duet comes to an end, where Crosby makes the claim; "Sooner or later you'll be screwing around", to which Aday responds, "I won't do that".

For the complete article, view: https://ultimateclassicrock.com/meat-loaf-i-would-do-anything-for-love

Where HAVE All the Cowboys Gone?

Album: This Fire (1996), In this song, Paula Cole plays a woman who is swept off her feet by a rugged cowboy in a '56 Chevy. She's happy to be his housewife while he provides for the family, but after a while lethargy sets in and her cowboy is more of a bum, hanging out at the bar while she takes care of the household. She no longer views him as her strong, supportive partner, who labored in the fields while she managed the household. Her 'cowboy' became another dependent, taking her for granted and showing no appreciation for her and their relationship has turned toxic. She can't help but wonder what happened to the tough, determined, stand- up guy she married.

In a Songfacts interview with Cole, she said: "It's so many things woven together: wit, irony, humor, melancholy, and gender role examination. It's all these things put together musically in this plaintive, Americana pop way."

'Cole is a staunch feminist and wrote this song with a sideways glance at gender stereotypes. The nuance of the song was lost on many listeners, who thought it was simply about a woman yearning for a manly man to take care of her.' *(https://www.songfacts.com/facts/paula-cole/where-have-all-the-cowboys-gone)*

Although twenty- five years have gone by since Cole raised the question, one has to wonder, where have all the cowboys gone? Do they still exist, or did their breed die out with the demise of Western Movies? Aside from riding horses and wearing ten gallon hats, chasing down wayward indians, becoming outlaws from justice and busting up saloons during illegitimate poker games, what exactly does a cowboy do? Who is the enigmatic cowboy? Https://www.history.com/topics/westward-expansion/cowboys had this to say about who our cowboys are and where they are today.

"Cowboys were mostly young men who needed cash. The average cowboy in the West made about $25 to $40 a month. In addition to herding cattle, they also helped care for horses, repaired fences and buildings, worked cattle drives and in some cases helped establish frontier towns. Cowboys occasionally developed a bad reputation for being lawless, and some were banned from certain establishments.

They typically wore large hats with wide brims to protect them from the sun, boots to help them ride horses and bandanas to guard them from dust. Some wore chaps on the outsides of their trousers to protect their legs from sharp cactus needles and rocky terrain. When they lived on a ranch, cowboys shared a bunkhouse with each other. For entertainment, some sang songs, played the guitar or harmonica and wrote poetry.

The cowboy played an important role during the era of U.S. westward expansion. Though they originated in Mexico, American cowboys created a style and reputation all their own. Throughout history, their iconic lifestyle has been glamorized in countless books, movies and television shows—but the rough, lonely and sometimes grueling work of a cowboy wasn't for the faint of heart.

In 1519, shortly after the Spanish arrived in the Americas, they began to build ranches to raise cattle and other livestock. Horses were imported from Spain and put to work on the ranches. Mexico's native cowboys were called vaqueros, which comes from the Spanish word vaca (cow). Vaqueros were hired by ranchers to tend to the livestock and were known for their superior roping, riding and herding skills. By the early 1700s, ranching made its way to present-day Texas, New Mexico, Arizona and as far south as Argentina. When the California missions started in 1769, livestock practices were introduced to more areas in the West.

During the early 1800s, many English-speaking settlers migrated to the West and adopted aspects of the vaquero culture, including their clothing style and cattle-driving methods. Cowboys came from diverse backgrounds and included African-Americans, Native Americans, Mexicans and settlers from the eastern United States and Europe.

In the mid-1800s, the United States built railroads that reached further west, and cowboys played a central part in the nation's "Manifest Destiny" as Westward expansion led to an ever-shifting frontier. Cowboys herded and rounded up livestock that were transported by rail around the country for sale.

To distinguish what cattle belonged to which ranch, cowboys would brand the animals by burning a special mark into their hides. It took between eight and 12 cowboys to move 3,000 head of cattle along cattle drives.

But by the 1890s, most of the land became privatized after feuds over land ownership were settled and the use of barbed wire became widespread. During the winter of 1886-1887, thousands of cattle died when temperatures reached well below freezing in parts of the West. Many scholars believe that this devastating winter was the beginning of the end for the cowboy era. Cattle drives continued, but on a smaller scale, up until the mid-1900s. Most cowboys gave up the open trail life and were hired by private ranch owners in the West.

Over the years, the number of working cowboys has declined, but the occupation isn't obsolete. The cowboy lifestyle and culture is still found in certain areas of the United States, albeit to a lesser degree than a century ago. Cowboys continue to help run large ranches in states like Texas, Utah, Kansas, Colorado, Wyoming and Montana.

According to the U.S. Bureau of Labor Statistics, in 2003 there were about 9,730 workers in the category "support activities for animal production," which included cowboys. These workers made an average of $19,340 per year. While opportunities may have shifted, the American cowboy is still very much a part of life in the American West.

Where IS the Beef?

Generations X and Y, along with many Baby Boomers, will most likely remember the Wendy's fast food chain commercials introduced in 1983 that featured a petite elderly woman peeking inside the buns of her burger from a competitor's kitchen and wondering out loud, " Where's the Beef?". The ads were meant to stake the claim that McDonalds and Burger King, while not specifically named, offer smaller burgers and a lesser quality of food in general. In the first commercial of its campaign, named "Fluffy Bun", actress Clara Peller is accompanied by two friends. They all order burgers, which are presented in large, fluffy buns, but lacking in a hearty meat patty, prompting Peller's verbal outburst. The catchphrase quickly caught on and although Wendy's has employed multiple other ad crusades over the years, "Where's The Beef" was brought back in 2011 due to its immense impact and success in word- of- mouth advertising.

Wikipedia defines *Where's the Beef* with a secondary meaning, as "an all-purpose phrase questioning the substance of an idea, event, or product." There is also an internet site called Schmoop.com that dedicates an entire installment to popular quotes, their origin and definition. It describes the use of the interjection as "anytime something lacks substance, and someone isn't happy about it; It means, 'I thought I was getting something better than this!'

"Also, if you were watching the 1984 Democratic debate (and who wasn't?), candidate Walter Mondale lobbed the catchphrase as an attack against his opponent."

While Mondale obviously wasn't reciting the query to promote Wendy's burgers, simply speaking the phrase was a huge tribute, as the debate would have been viewed by millions. Normally it would cost a company big bucks for an endorsement like that, but Wendy's gets plenty of free advertising!

Urbandictionary.com informs readers that following the debut of the commercial, with- in a year, "men began wearing t- shirts that boasted, 'Here's the beef!'", and it became "a sexual joke when a guy's d*ck isn't big enough". Sadly, I must admit that while having caddy conversations with my girlfriends, discussing our sordid pasts, I have regaled them with a story or two about a man whose lacking in the 'beef' department!

And one final mention on the topic of 'beef' appearing in the media... the roast beef joint, Arby's, now advertises with the phrase, " We have the beef." Is this a response to the question raised by Clara Peller for Wendy's? Or a pilfering of the catchphrase that made Peller so popular? I'm sure the lawyers assured the owners of Arby's that it's just different enough to make the cut.

Who Let the Dogs Out?

The obvious reference is to the annoying, obnoxious song "Who Let the Dogs Out", performed by the group Baha Men. The song, released in 2000, became the band's only hit and twenty years later, nailing down exactly where it came from is still anybody's guess. Apparently, a mish- mash of sources came together to create the catchy, all- be- it irritating tune. Mental floss article number 626928 tells readers "several people have come forward to claim ownership of the song's earworm of a chorus. A college football chant from the mid-1980s. A bunch of lyrics scribbled on a Little Caesars bread bag. A punk rock hairdresser named Keith. These are just a few of the seemingly random, but entirely vital, components of Baha Men's 2000 hit 'Who Let the Dogs Out'—a tune Rolling Stone once dubbed the third most annoying song of all time.

The slightly farcical, if hugely fascinating, narrative around the song is pored over in even greater detail in the 2019 documentary Who Let the Dogs Out. Directed by Brent Hodge (A Brony Tale, I Am Chris Farley), the hugely entertaining film sees artist/curator Ben Sisto deliver a TED Talk-style lecture about his eight-year journey to uncover the truth about the song's origins, interspersed with interviews with all the key players.

So who does Sisto, the self-described world's leading expert on 'Who Let the Dogs Out,' believe is most responsible for the song's success? 'Without a doubt, it's Steve Greenberg,' Sisto tells Mental Floss. 'It was his marketing acumen, industry ties, and honest dedication to the band that culminated in the track exploding.' " Nailing down the glorification of the tune is, apparently, simpler than discovering its true roots, but, what I still want to know is, what the heck does the song mean? What's letting the dog's out even mean? The best explanation I could find is from artist Anslem Douglas, who performed the original version of the song, released as "Doggie" in 1998. An interview featured on his site, Douglas himself admitted that the song has nothing to do with dogs and actually has a feminist theme. In an interview that was published on https://www.revelist.com/feminism/who-let-the-dogs-out/, he said:

"It's a man-bashing song. I'll tell you why. The lyric of the song says, 'The party was nice, the party was pumpin'.' When I said the word 'party' I was being metaphorical. It really means things were going great. The 'Yippie-Yi-Yo,' that's everybody's happy, right? 'And everybody was having a ball.' Life was going great. 'Until the men start the name-callin' / And then the girls respond to the call.' So the men started calling the women 'skank' and 'skettel,' every dirty word you can think of. The men started the name-calling and then the girls respond to the call. And then a woman shouts out, 'Who let the dogs out?' And we start calling men dogs. It was really a man-bashing song."

Admittedly, I never paid much attention to the lyrics with- in the verses of the song, and I didn't expect that there would be any substance to them. Consider me pleasantly surprised. Kudos to those Baha Men for being so progressive... I only wish they'd done it to a tune that didn't make my ears bleed! What I believed to be a mindless tune with nothing to offer but reverbs of barking dogs turned out to be advocacy for the women's movement. Who knew? Well, I guess, those who recited or revered the song knew. (Obviously). Still, I'm not moved to the point where I can let this *woof, woof* refrain become my new anthem. I'm sure the feminists of the world will understand.

What IS in His Kiss?

Sometimes it's desire, passion, lust, urgency, and at others it's just love, plain and simple, but at *all times*, what you'll find in his kiss is an incomprehensible amount of germs. After reading an article entitled, <u>80 Million Bacteria Sealed With A Kiss,</u> posted on biomedcentral.com, I can't imagine kissing my husband again without thinking about all the microscopic 'bugs' transferring from his saliva into my mouth. Yuck. If Betty Everette had this information back in 1964 when she made the hit, "The Shoop Shoop Song (It's In His Kiss)", she may have thought twice about celebrating his kiss!

"As many as 80 million bacteria are transferred during a 10 second kiss", reports the study published in the open access journal, Microbiome. The research also found that partners who kiss each other at least nine times a day share similar communities of oral bacteria. Wow! Yum!!

"The ecosystem of more than 100 trillion microorganisms that live in our bodies - the microbiome – is essential for the digestion of food, synthesizing nutrients, and preventing disease. It is shaped by genetics, diet, and age, but also the individuals with whom we interact. With the mouth playing host to more than 700 varieties of bacteria, the oral microbiota also appear to be influenced by those closest to us.

"Researchers from Micropia and TNO in the Netherlands studied 21 couples. The results showed that when couples intimately kiss at relatively high frequencies their salivary microbiota become similar. On average it was found that at least nine intimate kisses per day led to couples having significantly shared salivary microbiota.

"Lead author Remco Kort, from TNO's Microbiology and Systems Biology department and adviser to the Micropia museum of microbes, said: 'Intimate kissing involving full tongue contact and saliva exchange appears to be a courtship behavior unique to humans and is common in over 90% of known cultures. Interestingly, the current explanations for the function of intimate kissing in humans include an important role for the microbiota present in the oral cavity, although to our knowledge, the exact effects of intimate kissing on the oral microbiota have never been studied. We wanted to find out the extent to which partners share their oral microbiota, and it turns out, the more a couple kiss, the more similar they are.'

"In a controlled kissing experiment to quantify the transfer of bacteria, a member of each of the couples had a probiotic drink containing specific varieties of bacteria including Lactobacillus and Bifidobacteria. After an intimate kiss, the researchers found that the quantity of probiotic bacteria in the receiver's saliva rose threefold, and calculated that in total 80 million bacteria would have been transferred during a 10 second kiss."

If this article isn't enough to completely turn you off of open- mouthed kissing, another journalist shares what she believes you can expect reveal about your partner and your relationship with him/ her, just from the act of swapping spit.

Natasha Pelati on Pairedlife.com, <u>How to Tell If He Really Loves You</u>:

"A kiss can be magical and you can feel the electricity run through your body if there is an attraction. He doesn't have to be a great kisser for you to feel the love. If there is passion and he feels something for you, then you will feel it in his kiss.

"Kissing is practiced by all animals and it is a chemical reaction for them to find the perfect mate. Cats, dogs and other mammals lick each others' faces, while birds tap each others' beaks, and elephants put their trunks into each others' mouths. Humans are no different and the chemical reaction that is caused from a kiss can tell you if you have a matching partner or not. Obviously if a kiss is not great and there is no chemistry then you will know immediately. Scientists believe that saliva has hormones in it and serves many romantic purposes. Biological profiles connect mates together and they can be found through the saliva from a kiss.

"Should he be kissing you with his eyes open, then he is not passionate and can be a wanderer. A passionate kiss can be felt through your entire body and it should be done with closed eyes. "

… Ok, hold up, I need to chime in here because the statements made in this particular article seem like they are one person's opinion while they're being presented as if they are fact. *Some* evidence- based quips are cited, but other assertions, like the previous one regarding closed- eye- kisses, read like a personal experience that doesn't necessarily reflect the genuine truth. Speaking now from *my own* personal experience, your man opening his eyes during a kiss does *not* indicate a lack of love and affection. My husband and I have been together twenty years and the passion in our love- life hasn't diminished at all. Sometimes, because we share so much love between us, we'll hold each others gaze while locked in an intimate kiss, as if we're speaking to one another with a look that ultimately says 'I love you. I want you. I need you.' Him kissing me with his eyes wide open doesn't diminish the intensity of it at all.

I have no doubts what- so- ever that he and I feel the same profound love. I also know we can't be the only couple who sometimes ogle each other while we make out, so I'm guessing the writer of the excerpt above had a fairly foul romance with a guy who would eye- ball her when they were lip- locked. Let's see what other pearls of wisdom she has to offer as a result of her relationship experiences.

"If his kiss is sloppy and not very intimate and you can't feel anything from it, then he's not the guy for you. A bad kisser doesn't matter because bad or not, love can still be felt. Love is fantastic if it is with the right person and you just know and feel when it is real or true love."

I feel this is a decent appraisal of what can be represented in a kiss. Once a good friend of mine, who was male, decided that he had a crush on me and let me know about it. I never really thought of him in a romantic way, but I figured,'what the heck, it couldn't hurt to try'. Well it didn't quite hurt, but it was definitely *painful.* We kissed and it made me so unbelievably uncomfortable. The issue wasn't that he was appalling or anything like that; it was that he was more like a brother to me than anything else. Kissing him made me feel more sick to my stomach than anything else. That was the only 'chemical reaction' I had! Needless to say, I felt nothing encouraging from it and had to tell him that I was only interested in remaining friends. I have to agree with Pelati on this one, there is plenty to read into from a kiss that just doesn't jive.

"Besides the physical attributes, love can be shown in many ways and if he truly loves you he will be open and honest, loyal, respectful and loving to you all the time."

I agree with the honest, loyal and respectful comment, but as far as him being 'loving to you all the time'? That sounds bit unrealistic to me. I'm a total bitch to my old man sometimes, and his attitude sucks often enough. We are not *always* loving to each other... because we are human beings with human defects and a full range of emotions that aren't always kept in check. I'm thinking that if the author of this article doesn't lower her expectations, she'll never find a mate that's good enough for her whether the kisses are good or not!

Honestly, I'm wondering how old she is and how sheltered has she been? Oh, to be that naive... Admittedly, however, I tend to have a rather cynical outlook on certain matters. In this case, though, I don't think I'm just being pessimistic, simply realistic and practical. We take the good with the bad, right? There's sure to be a modicum of both in any and all relationships. I do agree with her idea that we can interpret the love in a kiss. I've felt it. There's no mistaking the passion behind mine and my husband's smooches, not to mention the chemical and physical reactions in our 'special' parts! Wait, is that love? Or just pure, unadulterated lust?

Why Do Fools Fall In Love?

Yes, this is the title of a hit song from the 1950s by Frankie Lymon & the Teenagers, as well as the name of the 1998 biographical movie about Lymon's life, starring Larenz Tate, Halle Berry and a host of popular actors and actresses. For this blurb, I wanted to try and answer the question of why love can make us do such foolish things! In the past, I've found myself inserting my foot in my mouth when faced with my crush. I know I'm not alone in this, and as a matter of fact, I found this article on line at www.elitedaily.com, entitled, "The Science Behind Why Falling In Love Really Does Make Us Stupid", written by Tara Suess:

"I consider myself to be a fairly intelligent person. I have a bachelor's degree, I was an (almost) straight-A student and I'll admit a little part of me dies inside when I overhear the improper use of the word 'literally'. But here's the thing: When I'm talking to my significant other, I suddenly become partially brain-dead and forget how to 'English'.

"Atrociously composed sentences will fly out of my mouth, such as, 'I sleeped well last night,' or 'I stealed some extra napkins.' The cringe-worthiness of these f*ckups is enough to make me want to crawl into a little ditch and stay there for a while. It's embarrassing, and it catches me completely off-guard because I don't usually make those kinds of mistakes, except when I'm talking to my S.O. What gives?

"As it turns out, I'm not the only one who struggles in the intelligence department when I'm preoccupied and thinking about that special someone. That crazy, mystical, whirlwind emotion called 'falling in love' may actually be responsible for the stupid things we hear ourselves say aloud around our crushes and significant others."

Something definitely happens to us when we're face- to- face with the one we love, especially during that initial 'honeymoon phase' when everything's fresh and new. Aren't convinced yet by Suess' personal musings? Well, she's got the science to back it up, too. You'll see! It's not just us!

"A 2013 study conducted by Dr. Henk van Steenbergan at Leiden University in the Netherlands, in conjunction with researchers at the University of Maryland, found that a budding romance or new love may actually temporarily diminish cognitive resources. Fifty-one participants who were involved in new romantic relationships (specifically those which were six months or less) were asked to differentiate important information from irrelevant information in as little time as possible. They completed this test after listening to romantic music, which was intended to remind them of their partners, thus eliciting feelings of love. The participants were also asked to complete a survey that assessed the strength and intensity of the love they felt for their significant others.

"The study found a correlation between poor performance on the test and how head-over-heels in love a person was feeling, regardless of gender. The less in love, the better they performed on the test. The more in love, the worse they fared. It seems that being loopy in love lessens our ability to focus and multitask because our S.O.s are taking up some vital brain space. It's sort of like how your computer slows down because you have too many windows and programs open at one time.

"When you fall in love, that person becomes pretty important and takes up a lot of your brain's 'hard drive' space. You can still function and get along fine, but everything might just run just a little slower. The good news? That head-over-heels loopiness can't last forever. In fact, Van Steenbergen concluded that in order for a relationship to survive long-term, regaining cognitive control is crucial. This makes sense.

"The honeymoon phase doesn't last forever. Eventually, the rose-colored glasses fade, and that 'drunk in love' feeling wears off. When your love matures to a steady flame instead of feeling like the crazy fireworks of a new relationship, your cognitive function should mellow out back to normal. In the meantime, however, you might just have to make do with your 'struck by Cupid's arrow' brain. So, falling in love can make us a little stupid. It's true, but it's probably not worst thing in the world…"

And there you have it. If you're like me, you've undergone bouts of verbal diarrhea as a symptom of your nervous energy when faced with someone you have a romantic interest in. Now we can take solace in knowing there *is* scientific proof that it's a result of biology and not due to a lack of smarts. Hopefully, though, armed with this new information, you don't blurb it all out after stumbling over your words the next time you encounter that hot body. The only downfall to knowing all of this? There's appears to be no excuse for fumbling through conversation with my husband. We've been together for twenty years! So maybe some of Suess's research is inconclusive. My hubby can still stir the butterflies in my stomach and make my mind swoon. The novelty may wear off for all couples, but fireworks aren't necessarily a thing of the past.

How Many Pickled Peppers Did Peter Piper Pick?

This age- old query first appeared over 200 years ago in 1813, in <u>Peter Piper's Practical Principles of Plain and Perfect Pronunciation,</u> by John Harris. The publication was a collection of tongue- twisters meant to help its readers with proper pronunciation of the english language. It's speculated, on the web- site, http://nurseryrhymesforbabies.com/tongue-twister-origin/, that the rhyme had been around for at least an entire generation prior to Harris' printing. Also, what you may not know is that tongue- twisters originated in the 1800s as a dictation tool to improve articulation for students. That didn't stop people from passing them around for their amusement, however. Bkacontent.com gives the complete 'Peter Piper' verse as:

"Peter Piper picked a peck of pickled peppers. Did Peter Piper pick a peck of pickled peppers? If Peter Piper picked a peck of pickled peppers, where's the peck of pickled peppers Peter Piper picked?"

I admit, I never heard it spoken with the second sentence, questioning whether he *did he pick a peck…* but I'm certainly no expert on it. To understand how much a 'peck' is and how many pickled peppers would fit in one, I went back to the first web- site mentioned, of nursery rhymes for babies. From this page, I learned not only the unit of measurement, but that Peter was an actual person; one, Pierre Poivre, who was a french missionary and then a botanist and horticulturalist in the 1700s. A clip from this site reads, "Even though Pierre was a plant expert and missionary, he became well known for stealing spices from Dutch traders. He would steal the spices and then use them to grow more spices in his own garden to sell at a more reasonable price to the average European colonists. At the time, pepper was the term used for all spices. So even though the tongue twister says he picked a peck of peppers, the peppers could really be anything from nutmeg to cinnamon. Unfortunately, the spice trading companies were smart enough to keep their spices from being stolen or bought and then used to grow more spices or peppers. This would have increased the supply of spices and lowered the price. The spice trade was carefully controlled to maximize profits. They would 'pickle' their spices by rubbing them with lime. The lime would keep the spices from germinating. The spices they sold would not grow more spices."

The only thing left to answer- how many peppers were actually picked? I took a swing at this one, too, and found that, "A peck is a 1/4 of a bushel, 2 dry gallons, 8 dry quarts, 16 dry pints. So a peck of peppers would yield somewhere between 10 and 14 pounds." Another fact is that about 5 medium sized peppers make   up   one pound. If you've ever wondered what the proper response was to the 100+ years old adage of how many pecks of peppers Peter picked, here's your answer; between 50 to 70 peppers.

Do You See What I See?

I really have no interest in delving into the story behind the beloved Christmas carol, so this entry is focused on the science behind people's different perceptions; physically, through site, but also philosophically, as in their outlook of the world around them. I wonder about color- blindness, if sight is effected by blue eyes, male or female vantages, and also how someone's individual background influences how they view everything around them. I have hazel eyes, my husband has baby- blues and our daughters inherited his genes and both have bright aquamarines while our son's irises are dark brown like my oldest daughter (whose eyes match *her* dad's). It drives me crazy because it's a rare occasion that three of us agree on the hue of something we're looking at. It's like we aren't even seeing the same thing; I call it blue, one of them says it green and another claims it's somewhere in between the two. It's crazy to me, so, I looked for the science behind it.

"While eye color doesn't affect how people see something, the color of someone's eyes can cause them to have different sight abilities in various lighting conditions. The melanin concentration in the pigment of the iris cells acts as a way to protect the iris from higher sunlight by spreading the light out. Someone with darker eyes has a higher amount and density of melanin. This means that in bright sunlight, the melanin reflects light inside the eye and they experience less problems with glare from the sun.

"Melanin acts as a kind of protector, spreading the light rays away from the iris. This does give them better contrast ability in these conditions. An example where darker eye color is an advantage might be in the glare of headlights when driving at night.

"People that have less melanin tend to have lighter colored eyes and therefore they lack the protection from the brighter light and can experience more discomfort of glare and less contrast. While the color of someone's eyes does not directly affect how they see things, the lighting conditions can be a secondary level that can affect sight." (https://www.konnecthq.com/eye-color/)

So, the short answer is, no, eye color itself doesn't determine the colors we see. Color is processed through the retinal cones of the eye, according to http://scienceline.ucsb.edu/. " The iris is 'pigmented' (has color) and therefore blocks light. This funnels the light into the pupil which will send it to retinal cells for processing by the brain. The color of the iris has no effect on how the light is processed by the retinal cells though it may affect the chance of eye disease."

That covers my investigation into whether eye- color effects our color perception. Now onto the more abstract query of whether a person's life experience is relevant to their outlook on what goes on around them. This comes from a post on medium.com by Will Campbell.

"There are some things that directly influence how we form our Worldviews and others which do so indirectly. So, what are these things and how do they participate in forming our Worldview, and our identity?

"When you sit down to really think about it, you would be able to easily identify what these things are. It is rather intuitive once you actually toss the idea around in your head. This is probably the simplest aspect of understanding what Worldviews are and where they come from. As we go through the list, it is important to note that we might be able to identify any number of things which influence our Worldview. However, most all individual things can be categorized into what is going to be identified here. Some might be able to reorganize or perhaps change the labels of these things, but this list seems the simplest yet most comprehensive way to explain this subject.

- Family- Our parents will instill in us those values and principles that they hold dear and will raise us to believe as they believe. They teach us what is right and what is wrong, and they explain the narrative story of humanity and the cosmos to us as we ask questions and experience new discoveries. Where we see our parents agree or disagree with aunts and uncles, as our grandparents tell us the stories of their lives, and as our older brother and sisters hassle us and play with us, they all impact how we form our Worldview. While the impact our family has on our Worldview is quite significant, it is not the only thing that forms both our identity as well as the

Worldview which grounds it. Beyond immediate family and relatives from our youth on into adulthood, we must include our spouses as well. As we begin to form our own families, experiencing what it is like to be our parents by being parents ourselves, our Worldview starts to haves its practical application challenged or validated. These experiences, along with the sense of duty and obligation to raise our children in truth, all impact our Worldviews in ways that nothing else can.

- Friends- The next influencer is our circle of friends as we grow up and even into our adulthood. Those outside of family with whom we form special bonds of friendship (can) impact our Worldview more dramatically than family depending on our relationship with parents and relatives. Our friends tend to impact our Worldview from something of a "Peer Pressure" standpoint. This can be both positive and negative depending on what they are trying to influence you to be. our personality can allow friends to be more significant influencers, or less significant. If we are strong willed and bold, then we will impact our friends more than they will impact us. If we are more easily swayed, perhaps more on the shy or timid side, we'll adjust our own self to meet what our friends seem to expect out of us.

- Community- Culture has the most significant impact on us growing up, and has the most significant sway on our Ethic and more superficial levels of Worldview formation. However, depending on the traditions within the culture we are raised, other elements such as the Narrative story of the Worldview can be formed by the telling of the history of the community within which we are raised. The common customs and courtesies of the community will impact how we behave when interacting with others, and the "social norms" of the community will affect what we perceive to be the normal course of human affairs. The most common influencer of our Worldview within the community is that desire we have to "fit in". As we begin to venture out on our own, being exposed to other cultures and communities, again depending on our personality, other cultures and communities may begin to influence us.

- Educators- Depending on where we are educated and what the Worldview is that is being taught, we will find ourselves adopting whatever Worldview the educators have. This has a stronger influence over our Worldview formation than family and friends however, that can be impacted by our personality as well. But regardless, education is what provides us with answers to various questions we may have had, or never even thought of asking, or ever really cared to. Again, depending on how healthy and strong our relationship is with our parents and relatives, whatever Worldview is being taught by our educators will become the Worldview we start off with in the world.

- Popular Influence- As we get older, we all go through something of a rebellious streak it seems. Again, depending on our personality, and how healthy and strong our relationships are with family and friends, the next most significant influencer is that which is popular at the time. This influencer is more along the lines of popular culture, entertainment, media personalities, and those we look up to.

- Life Experiences- Another major influencer of our Worldview acts on us in more of an indirect way. This influencer works on us seemingly in the background. Other times, it slaps us in the face, devastating us to our core, and causing a dramatic transformation in our identity and how we view the world. As we go through life from childhood on into adulthood, the things we live out and experience will either validate the beliefs instilled in us by our family, friends, and community, or will absolutely decimate them. Life experiences may not be the most significant influencer, but it is the validator of what we have been influenced to believe. There are times where traumatic experiences can shock us into complete denial of reality, shaking us to our very core. Other times we have subtle discoveries happen that poke holes in what we thought was true. No matter the case, what we experience in life will have either a positive or negative impact on our Worldview.

- Self- The final influencer is the one you might have been tempted to put first on the list. We would all like to think that we've come to form our own Worldview alone. The influence of our own conscious thinking on our beliefs is always actively involved, however, it is not often that we engage our thinking down to the "deeper" level of the philosophical questions of God, Man, and the Cosmos. Others just have that personality that leads them down the path of questioning everything. In the end, we all ultimately determine what Worldview we will follow, either by letting others form it for us, or by doing so ourselves.

- Bringing it all together- What we can see throughout this process of listing the various influencers of our Worldview is that the formation of our Worldview is a life-long process. As we experience new things and witness events we hadn't experienced yet, our Worldview can change both in small ways, and in transformative ways. We all begin the Worldview Formation process in our childhood. This is where our parents and family have the greatest impact on how we form our Worldviews early in life. The more our parents put into helping us build our Worldview to match theirs, the stronger a bond we form with them. As we ask our parents and grandparents questions about life, if they all provide the same answers, and show us how they came to those conclusions, we become quite strong in our identity and become more stable in our life. . If we can't get our answers from them, or they are not willing to provide them, we begin to look elsewhere.

"As we start to attend school at an early age, we are not so much impacted by our teachers as we are by our peers. As we interact with other students, and become exposed to their ideas (simple as they may be), those kids we come to admire or look up to will start to influence us. So, we see how important teachers and friends are at the earliest stage of our Worldview development, and how dramatically important the active role of our parents in forming our Worldviews is.

"Once we get into our teenage years, community and popular culture begin to play their part. Our parents are still the most important and significant formers. Where they fail, we will fill the gap by turning to popular media, entertainment, movie and music stars, and other popular figures in the culture.

"This then continues on into our young adult life as we move out of the home and into the 'real world.' As we begin to experience life's stresses of rent and bills, getting to class on our own and balancing our schedules, we lose the extra time we squandered in our youth as our days are filled with study or work. That is where educators continue to have significant influence alongside our friends and peer groups, and our exposure to other cultures and Worldviews on the job site or in the college classroom. This is where our sources for information become the biggest influencers of our Worldview formation.

"As we get challenged in courses by Ivory Tower professors, and all the books we read, or as we deal with our bosses and senior employees at work, all of these things begin to rapidly solidify the Worldview we carry for most our lives. Then life experiences begin to settle in.

"We all have different life experiences, and we are not all raised the same. Not all of us go to school or find work. We do not all fall into the sway of Hollywood and political movements. However, this pattern does tend to play itself out for the average everyday "Joe Schmo" type. Life Experience and the Self is what it ultimately comes down to. Parents can influence, Family can, long-time Friends can, Popular Influence, various information sources, all of these things continually impact us. In the end, it all comes down at some point in time to the individual person, sitting down one day and finally asking his or her self the questions of life, and figuring out what they really believe."

Wow, that was a lot of information, but I appreciate the clarity and specificity of the message. I didn't exactly realize how many things can influence a person's outlook on the world, but that article certainly laid it all out, pretty straight- forward. My family was, and is, pretty close, so I imagine they had quite a bit to do with forming my take on things and instilling a value system. One thing I can say for sure, they taught me, ' family first' and not to settle for less. I'm not exactly aware what I've taken from the friendships I had when I was younger, but as an adult, I've formed relationships with people who've shown me unconditional love and teachers who encouraged me to reach my potential. If anything, society and those in the limelight showed me what I did NOT want to become and somehow pushed me to embrace my individuality in opposition of conforming to the societal norms. Whether it was about rebelling against the expectations I felt were put on me or because I was self- conscious with low self- esteem, and went to the extreme in the opposite direction of what I thought was 'conforming' to build an imaginary wall between me and everyone else, I was 25 when I finally came into my own.

My parents definitely instilled values and morals in me when I was young. They taught me that one needed to work hard to get to where you want to be and that sometimes it's necessary to do things you really don't want to do because that's just life. Aside from the positive traits they passed on to me, though, I carry a lot of baggage from growing up in my house. There was a level of dysfunction that not only molded my mind, but also warped my personality. My experiences has provided me with a pretty cynical attitude, but they are also responsible for an enormous amount of growth in me, mentally and emotionally. I've had to learn to undo some of the behaviors I developed as an adolescent that had become self- defense mechanisms, like hiding my feelings and not sharing my thoughts. Although family dynamics may have contributed to my most unhealthy habits, it also provided me with the drive and strength I needed to get past my negative tendencies and replace them with more healthy practices that allow me to live life on life's terms.

Must What Goes Up, Come Down?

This popular expression, "What goes up must come down", is attributed to Sir Isaac Newton and his Universal Law of Gravitation, with which he settles the query with a resounding, Yes; what goes up must, inevitably, come down. The story, as I recall from my elementary school years, goes something like: Isaac Newton was sitting under an apple tree when an apple fell on his head. The apple falling caused him to suddenly conclude that *something* must have been pulling the apple down to Earth... After some time, thinking and theorizing, he then came up with the Law of Gravity. While some of the specifics have certainly been invented, Newton *does* credit an apple tree as his inspiration.

Britannica.com defines The Law of Gravity as such 'that any particle of matter in the universe attracts any other with a force varying directly as the product of the masses and inversely as the square of the distance between them... Newton put forward the law in 1687 and used it to explain the observed motions of the planets and their moons, which had been reduced to mathematical form by Johannes Kepler early in the 17th century.

"Newton discovered the relationship between the motion of the Moon and the motion of a body falling freely on Earth. By his dynamical and gravitational theories, he explained Kepler's laws and established the modern quantitative science of gravitation. Newton assumed the existence of an attractive force between all massive bodies, one that does not require bodily contact and that acts at a distance. By invoking his law of inertia (bodies not acted upon by a force move at constant speed in a straight line), Newton concluded that a force exerted by Earth on the Moon is needed to keep it in a circular motion about Earth rather than moving in a straight line. He realized that this force could be, at long range, the same as the force with which Earth pulls objects on its surface downward."

Being a laywoman as far as physics is concerned, the science is a bit lost on me, yet not just one musician but 11 different bands, at least, have found Newton's work so intriguing, they recorded songs with the line, "What Goes Up Must Come Down", from a 2020 spoken word piece by Yellow Days, back fifty- two years to a Blood, Sweat and Tears ditty, "Spinning Wheel" from 1969. It is plausibly the most popular of all eleven plus songs. This oldie but goodie features vocalist David Clayton-Thomas, along with other original band members, Al Kooper, Jim Fielder, Fred Lipsius, Randy Brecker, Jerry Weiss, Dick Halligan, Steve Katz and Bobby Colomby, who made the words come to life on the stage at Woodstock in 1970. If you were born before the 21st Century, you know this tune. The lyrics, according to musixmatch.com, are:

What goes up must come down

Spinning Wheel got to go 'round

Talkin' 'bout your troubles

It's a cryin' sin

Ride a painted pony

Let the Spinning Wheel spin

You got no money, you got no home

Spinning Wheel all alone

Talkin' 'bout your troubles and you

You never learn

Ride a painted pony

Let the Spinning Wheel turn

Did you find your directing sign

On the straight and narrow highway

Would you mind a reflecting sign?

Just let it shine within your mind

And show you the colors that are real

Someone is waiting just for you

Spinning Wheel spinning true

Drop all you troubles by the river side

Is Sunday Morning Easy?

For forty- four years, the words from this song, that 'I'm easy like Sunday morning' have stooped multiple people trying to decipher its meaning. It's not exactly one of those lines that adopted itself to regular dialogue, but after four decades, it still stumps the masses. What the hell is *easy like Sunday morning*? The only application of the word easy that I know of, outside of something effortless, is using it to describe a loose and promiscuous female, but that just didn't make sense here. As I often find, the simplest explanation is usually he most accurate. After reading the following excerpt, it seemed the answer should have been quite obvious, but has eluded me since I first heard it.

"Commodores lead singer Lionel Richie wrote this song in 1977. In this song, Richie sings about giving up on a relationship because it's bringing him down. He feels liberated after the breakup and has a sense of calm that's 'easy like Sunday morning.' The song is often misinterpreted as a sweet love song. 'A lot of ballads, the song would just end, but we wanted the guitar solo to take it to another level of intensity. So that was basically the inspiration behind it.' Richie explained to Spin magazine the 'Easy' lyric: "'Easy like Sunday morning' applies to anybody who lives in a small Southern town. Small Southern towns die at 11:30 p.m. Saturday night. They roll up the sidewalk. So I kind of got that from my own experiences - that was Lionel Richie from Tuskegee, Alabama, where there is no such thing as four-in-the-morning partying."

Cool facts about the song "Easy"; 1. This was a cover by Faith No More, 2. It was used in commercials for Levis, 3. In 2016, Lionel Richie sang this song in three DIRECTV commercials with the lyrics altered to "It's Peyton on Sunday Morning." 4. Sky Ferreria sings it as Baby's mother in the 2017 movie *Baby Driver.*

(https://www.songfacts.com/facts/commodores/easy)

I guess the long and short of it is that there's no profound or secret message behind being 'easy like Sunday morning'. If Richie had just written it as *easy- going,* it would've saved me from any confusion and I would've known that he simply implies that he's feeling mellow, laid- back, at ease, like one might on a lazy Sunday morning.

Do You, (You!), Feel like I Do?

Do you recognize the refrain? This song has been around for sometime, in that sound exclusive to classic rock solo artist Peter Frampton. His album, <u>The Camel</u>, introduced this golden oldie in 1973, and it was an instant hit. Despite its popularity, this tune is said to have no deep or profound meaning, as songfacts.com discovered in an interview with the band. The journalist summarized it on the site;

"This song is about a hangover. Frampton would often write from experience, and at the time he was experiencing the effects of a night of drinking. When he woke up that morning there was a wine glass by his bed, and he wondered how it got there ('Whose wine? What wine? Where the hell did I dine?').

"Still hungover, Frampton went to rehearsal and somehow remembered some chords he was playing the night before on his acoustic guitar. The band hashed out the tune and told Frampton to come up with some lyrics, to which he replied, 'I can't, I have a really bad hangover.' His bandmates told him to just write about that, which he did."

Peter Frampton's celebrated sound may be original, and his hollywood success uncommon amongst us lay-people, but there are some things he shares with every human being; how he experiences 'touch'. We concur that everyone is different. We all have our own set of DNA codes, individual cells, particular looks, even a unique set of fingerprints, yet did you know that also specific to us is our sense of touch and yes, also how we *feel* emotions and process information? In wondering, "do others feel in the same way I do?", I began to ponder whether pain is also relative. There is, of course, a whole neuroscience dedicated to this subject, and I learned something I found quite interesting; that in some cases, others don't necessarily *feel* like I do.

First, let's go over the science of experiencing physical feelings and of touch, as covered at https://askabiologist.asu.edu/explore/how-do-we-feel-touch:

"(Our) sensory receptors respond to a specific type of touch, they all act in the same way when they are activated. As part of the nervous system, these receptors will fire an action potential. Action potentials are signals sent by the special cells, called neurons, that make up the nervous system. They are used to share many different kinds of information within the nervous system. Action potentials from all of these receptors will send signals to both the spinal cord and the brain.

"Neuroscientists *still* aren't sure how signals from these receptors are changed into information that a person can understand. For example, when you are tickled versus poked, you know right away what happened. But how does the brain let you know whether it's a tickle or a poke based on only a few action potentials? Scientists continue to study this question."

It may not be as clear from the data above, but touch and pain *is* relative, and dependant on much more than nerve endings and receptors, although these are the basic fundamentals to the sense of touch. When it comes to pain, research is much more conclusive. We all experience it a bit differently. How we *feel* it depends on how we are *feeling* mentally. The excerpt below comes from an article, <u>The Neuroscience of Touch and Pain,</u> on brainfacts.org.

"If you and your friend both stub the same toe on the same door jamb, you'll probably experience the pain differently. Pain depends both on the strength of the stimulus and the emotional state and setting in which the injury occurs. When messages arrive in the cortex, the brain can process them differently depending on whether you had a good day or just broke up with your girlfriend.

"The cortex sends pain messages to the periaqueductal gray matter, which activates pathways that modulate pain. Pathways send messages to networks that release endorphins — natural opioids that act like the pain reliever morphine. Adrenaline produced during emotionally stressful situations also serves as a pain reliever. Releasing these chemicals helps regulate and reduce pain by intercepting signals traveling through the spinal cord and brainstem.

"Although everyone has these brain circuits, how well they work and how sensitive they are influence how much pain someone feels. It's why some people develop chronic pain that regular treatment can't relieve. Endorphins act at multiple types of opioid receptors in the brain and spinal cord. Doctors can deliver opioid drugs to the spinal cord before, during, and after surgery to reduce pain. Scientists are studying ways to electrically stimulate the spinal cord to relieve pain while avoiding the harmful effects of long-term opioid use.

"No single brain area is responsible for pain and itch perception. Emotional and sensory components create a mosaic of activity influencing how we perceive pain. Some successful treatments target the emotional component like meditation, hypnosis, cognitive behavioral therapy, and the controlled use of cannabis. Patients with chronic pain still feel pain, but it doesn't "hurt" as much. Brain imaging shows that cannabis suppresses activity in only a few pain areas, mostly the limbic system, the brain's emotional center. Scientists don't fully understand how these therapies work yet."

I can't claim to fully understand the concepts laid out above, but the point certainly came across; when it comes to pain and touch, as much depends on the impact of the physical experience of pain as it does on our emotional state. That would explain why one day I can bang my knee on the corner of my coffee table and laugh it off, while on another day I can whack it in exactly the same manner and burst into tears! The science makes sense, and I have my own experiences to back it up, I just never really put two and two together until now. It feels like I just got a little heads up for the next time a piece of furniture jumps out at me... I can tap into those coping skills I've got for self- soothing and enhance my threshold for pain.

Did Mary Really Have a Little Lamb?

Yes, there was a Mary and she did, in fact have a little lamb, however, I had no idea it would be such a story of felicity and scandal! Here is the whole, spanish novela- type story as relayed through a Dec 19, 2017 article, penned by Andrew Amelinckx at Modernfarmer.com:

"*Spoiler: its fleece *was* as white as snow. The nursery rhyme, which was was first published in 1830, is based on an actual incident involving Mary Elizabeth Sawyer, a woman born in 1806 on a farm in Sterling, Mass. In 1815, Mary, then nine, was helping her father with farm chores when they discovered a sickly newborn lamb in the sheep pen that had been abandoned by its mother. After a lot of pleading, Mary was allowed to keep the animal, although her father didn't hold out much hope for its survival. Against the odds, Mary managed to nurse the lamb back to health.

'In the morning, much to my girlish delight, it could stand; and from that time it improved rapidly. It soon learned to drink milk; and from the time it would walk about, it would follow me anywhere if I only called it,' Mary would later write in the 1880s, many decades after the incident. And, yes, the lamb would indeed follow her wherever she went and did have a fleece as white as snow.

"Sometime later, it's uncertain exactly when, Mary was heading to school with her brother when the lamb began following them. The siblings apparently weren't trying very hard to prevent the lamb from tagging along, even hauling it over a large stone fence they had to cross to get to Redstone School, the one-room schoolhouse they attended. Once there, Mary secreted her pet under her desk and covered her with a blanket. But when Mary was called to the front of the class to recite her lessons, the lamb popped out of its hiding place and, much to Mary's chagrin and to the merriment of her classmates, came loping up the aisle after her. The lamb was shooed out, where it then waited outside until Mary took her home during lunch. The next day, John Roulstone, a student a year or two older, handed Mary a piece of paper with a poem he'd written about the previous day's events. You know the words:

"Mary had a little lamb;

Its fleece was white as snow;

And everywhere that Mary went,

The lamb was sure to go.

It followed her to school one day,

Which was against the rule;

It made the children laugh and play

To see a lamb at school.

And so the teacher turned it out;

But still it lingered near,

And waited patiently about

Till Mary did appear.

"The lamb grew up and would later have three lambs of her own before being gored to death by one of the family's cows at age four. Another tragedy struck soon after when Roulstone, by then a freshman at Harvard, died suddenly at age 17.

"Here's where the controversy begins. In 1830, Sarah Josepha Hale, a renowned writer and influential editor (she's also known as the "Mother of Thanksgiving" for helping making the day a holiday), published Poems for Our Children, which included a version of the poem. According to Mary herself, Roulstone's original contained only the three stanzas, while Hale's version had an additional three stanzas at the end. Mary admitted she had no idea how Hale had gotten Roulstone's poem. When asked, Hale said her version, titled "Mary's Lamb," wasn't about a real incident, but rather something she'd just made up. Soon the residents of Sterling and those of Newport, New Hampshire, where Hale hailed from, were arguing about the poem's provenance – something they continued to do for years. In the 1920s, by which time both Mary Sawyer and Sarah Hale were dead, none other than Henry Ford, the man who revolutionized the auto industry, leapt into the fray. The inventor sided with Mary's version of events. He ended up buying the old schoolhouse where the lamb incident took place and moved it to Sudbury, Mass., then published a book about Mary Sawyer and her lamb. In the end, it seems the most logical explanation is that Hale simply added the additional stanzas to Roulstone's original (which she'd probably gotten wind of at some point).

"In the end, the nursery rhyme took on a life of its own after it was set to music. It became wildly popular beginning in the mid-1800s. The poem even became the first audio recording in history when Thomas Edison recited it on his newly invented phonograph in 1877 in order to see if the machine actually worked. It did… Back in Sterling, Mass., they continue to celebrate Mary Sawyer. There's a statue of the famous lamb in town, and a restored version of Mary's home (the original was destroyed by a pair of arsonists back in 2007). Her descendants continue to farm the land that gave birth to the most famous nursery rhyme of all time."

Imagine? That cherished rhyme has survived for 200 years, being recited and passed on from generations of parents and grandparents, onto the next era. Who knew the controversy surrounding its origin? Admittedly, I did not. I've heard the rhyme innumerous times, as well as retold it in a sing- song voice to my own children, nieces and nephews. Thankfully, I didn't have the answer then to what became of Mary's little lamb.

When my kids, now adolescents, were younger, they even learned to toot out the melody in grade school, on those gawd- awful air instruments commonly known as *recorders*. Quite often, it's one of the first melodies teachers use to get their students fluent on the piano. If Mary Sawyers' descendants and kin could earn a nickel for everytime the poem was repeated, they'd have been billionaires by now; one nickel at a time!!

What's 'Sweet Caroline' to the Boston Red Socks?

I am not a baseball buff, although, being a resident of the suburbs north of Boston makes the Red Sox my team by default. I really don't follow any sports at all, but I am aware that 'Sweet Caroline' plays at Fenway Park during home games, prompting fans around the bleachers to sing from the top of their lungs. I could never figure out what relevance the song had to the Boston Red Socks team or to the game being played on the diamond, (other than the singer being named Niel *Diamond).* I knew a sir name couldn't be the connection, so what was it?! Then I found out it there was really no explicit reasoning behind how the song came to be the team's anthem, other than a superstitious emcee and enthusiastic vice president of public affairs.

'It all started with a baby named Caroline. During a 1997 game at Fenway, Amy Tobey, who was one of the employees in charge of music at the ballpark during that season, played "Sweet Caroline" because someone she knew had recently given birth to a baby of that name, according to MLB.com.

Tobey became superstitious about its use over the next several years, only playing the song between the seventh and ninth innings when the Red Sox were winning the game. In that way, the song served the same purpose as "Gino Time," a video mashup of American Bandstand dancers grooving to the Bee Gees' "You Should Be Dancing" that started playing at the TD Garden (then known as the Fleet Center) in 1996, but only during the last TV timeout of games the Celtics were almost assured to win.

But when Dr. Charles Steinberg became the Red Sox executive vice president of public affairs in 2002, he quickly seized on the song as an integral part of the Fenway experience. As the song's popularity at Fenway Park began to grow, its creator became increasingly tied to the team — and to Boston itself. Neil Diamond cemented that tie in 2007 by revealing that the song was about New England's own Caroline Kennedy, for whom he performed it on her 50th birthday. Diamond has backed away from that claim in recent years, saying that the song was about his then-wife, Marsha, during an appearance on Today in 2014.

"I was writing a song in Memphis, Tennessee, for a session. I needed a three-syllable name. The song was about my wife at the time — her name was Marsha — and I couldn't get a 'Marsha' rhyme."

(Maybe he said that to get out of the doghouse, I don't know). Regardless of the song's inspiration, it has staying power as part of quintessential Boston culture. In 2013, Diamond appeared at Fenway to perform the song after the Boston Marathon bombings, and said he would donate royalties from the song to One Fund Boston. Other baseball teams around the country also played it in solidarity with Boston in the aftermath of the attacks. Even in its adopted home ballpark, however, "Sweet Caroline" doesn't enjoy universal appeal.

Local baseball purists and music fans are some of the song's biggest detractors, as Geoff Edgers found out in his 2013 Boston Globe piece on the song's Fenway ubiquity. Among the Caroline haters were radio host Tony Massarotti ("I hate the 'tradition'"), Globe columnist Bob Ryan (he called the playing of the song during Boston's 69-93 season in 2012 a "national disgrace"), and Buffalo Tom lead singer Bill Janovitz, who, when asked what song should replace "Sweet Caroline," simply responded: "Anything."

Some of the grievances stem from the baseball purist's notion that "Sweet Caroline" is a bellwether of "pink hat" fandom — in other words, baseball treated as a social outing, not as a competitive game. Edgers, a veteran music journalist who now works for The Washington Post, was especially harsh in his assessment of the song's musical qualities, writing, "It's a largely forgettable, three-minute slab of Velveeta with a distinct creepiness ('Warm, touchin' warm') when you consider it was written by Neil Diamond, pushing 30 at the time, about Caroline Kennedy, then a preteen."

After the 2012 season, the team's worst record this millennium, Red Sox brass briefly discussed removing the song from the park playlist, according to The Globe. But in the end, tradition won out. The next season, the Red Sox won the World Series, and the times were once again "So good! so good!'"

(https://www.boston.com/sports/boston-red-sox/2017/10/08/how-sweet-caroline-became-fenways-beloved-and-detested-ballpark-anthem)

Although I'm with all those who find the song less than stellar and the chorus an attack on humans' peace of mind, I support the tradition of blasting the stadium with it. After all, it has been the drill for 20+ years.

When is it Time to Make the Donuts?

In the early 1980s, Michael Vale became the face of Dunkin' Donuts as "Fred the Baker", a middle- aged bakery chef who schlepped himself into the bakery during the wee hours of the morning to crank out endless amounts of sweet, ring-shaped, fried cakes ready for glazing, frosting and sprinkling. His catch-phrase, 'Time to make the donuts', became so popular that it's now a euphemism for going to work or beginning any job or task, especially the medial. The donut itself, a very simple pastry, has earned nation-wide recognition, with the first Friday in June having been designated *Donut Day* for eighty decades now. Wikipedia explains that in the early 1900s, it was a historical time for donut making:

"National Doughnut Day started in 1938 as a fund raiser for Chicago's The Salvation Army. Their goal was to help those in need during the Great Depression, and to honor The Salvation Army 'Lassies' of World War I, who served doughnuts to soldiers. Doughnut Dollies were women volunteers of the Salvation Army, who traveled to France in 1918 to support US soldiers... Soon after the US entrance into World War I in 1917, The Salvation Army sent a fact-finding mission to France. The mission concluded that the needs of U.S. enlisted men could be met by canteens/social centers termed 'huts' that could serve baked goods, (such as donuts), provide writing supplies and stamps, and provide a clothes-mending service. Typically, the six staff members per hut would include four female volunteers who could 'mother' the boys. These huts were established by The Salvation Army in the United States near army training centers."

Hence, the popularity of the donut, and FYI, it was 1950 when the first Dunkin Donuts, DD, was opened. The now internationally recognized chain debuted in Quincy, Massachusetts, which is about thirty- five miles from where I grew up. I'm not sure what time it was supposed to be that Fred arrived on set in the DD commercial, but in real life, bakers can begin their mornings as early as 3 or 4am. It was certainly implied by the way he slowly shuffled into the simulated kitchen, still sleepy- eyed and dragging his feet, that he was setting up shop before dawn,.

Regarding Fred, a.k.a. Michael Vale, Mentalfloss.com offers up "12 things you might not know about the man behind the mug", an informative account of Vale's little- known history:

"1. HE WAS A CLASSICALLY TRAINED ACTOR

2. HE PLAYED A CAB DRIVER IN 'A HATFUL OF RAIN'

3. HE WAS IN 'MARATHON MAN'

4. HE WAS A REGULAR ON *BROADWAY*

5. YOU PROBABLY CAUGHT HIM ON ONE OF YOUR FAVORITE CHILDHOOD SHOWS

6. HE PITCHED COTTAGE CHEESE BEFORE HE PITCHED DONUTS

7. HE PLAYED 'FRED THE BAKER' FOR 15 YEARS

8. VALE WASN'T THE DUNKIN' MARKETING TEAM'S FIRST CHOICE

9. FRED'S CATCHPHRASE TOOK ON A LIFE OF ITS OWN

10. VALE ONLY EVER MADE ONE DONUT

11. FRED'S RETIREMENT WAS KIND OF A BIG DEAL*

12. VALE PASSED AWAY IN 2005

*Apparently, when DD decided to squash the 'Time to make the donuts' commercial, along with Michael Vale's character, Fred, they polled consumers for their reaction prior to pulling the plug. The feedback indicated so much love for Fred that the corporation decided to celebrate his retirement with a parade through the streets of Boston, Massachusetts and a 'free donut day'. That was in 1997, sixteen years after the launch of the ad campaign. Today, 'Fred's' legacy lives on through his signature remark, which is printed on every DD donut box.

How Much Wood Would a Woodchuck, Chuck, If a Woodchuck Could Chuck Wood?

According to the age- old tongue- twister, the proper response to this question is 'a woodchuck would chuck as much wood as a woodchuck could chuck (if a woodchuck could chuck wood)'. But just how much wood would that be? Wouldn't you know, someone actually took the time to figure that out? Turns out, it's not only a phrase to get you tongue- tied, but it originated as lyrics to a song:

"The *Woodchuck* tongue twister is from the refrain of the 'Woodchuck Song,' written by Robert Hobart Davis and Theodore F. Morse. The song debuted in an American summer hit comedy musical *The Runaways*, which had a run of 167 performances between May and October in 1903 at New York City's Casino Theater. The song was sold to consumers as sheet music. It was produced performed by Ragtime Bob Roberts, featuring actress/singer/comedian Fay Templeton, and recorded on Edison wax cylinders, which predated flat phonograph records..

"In 1988, state wildlife conservation officer Richard Thomas of New York attempted to figure out just how much a wood a woodchuck could chuck, if a woodchuck was capable of doing so and had the inclination. Woodchucks don't actually chuck (throw) wood, of course, but, since they are a burrowing rodent, they *do* know how to toss around some dirt. So Thomas took to calculating a typical size of a woodchuck burrow, which consists of three rooms and a tunnel running through it that is roughly six inches wide and extends 25 to 30 feet. He determined that 35 square feet of soil needed to be excavated to create such a burrow. Knowing that a cubic foot of soil weighs 20 pounds, he calculated that a woodchuck could chuck 700 pounds of dirt a day. This calculation led Mr. Thomas, by extension, to an answer to what was then an 85-year-old question. Should a woodchuck be so inclined, Thomas concluded, " he could chuck about 700 pounds of wood." (https://www.thoughtco.com/tongue-twisters-woodchuck-1210400)

For an idea of what that may look like, imagine putting a small pine tree through a wood chipper. If the tree was about fifteen feet tall and maybe a foot around... that might yield you about 700 pounds of lumber. If woodchucks only gnawed on wood, rather than digging up or flinging wood embedded in the soil, they might be in business!

Part Two

Miscellaneous References

Blondes Have More Fun, But Brunettes Get Sh*t Done

As a card- holding buxom and intelligent brunette, I have to agree... Dark- haired beauties take the cake when compared to our tow- headed counterparts, but this article I found at elitedaily.com, named, <u>The Platinum Effect: 7 Reasons Why Blondes Actually Have More Fun,</u> written by Izabella Zaydenberg in 2015, provides some possibly biased information to explain why it's more exciting to travel through life with sun-kissed tresses:

"Blondes? Well, we're usually on the butt end of a joke. Phrases like "dumb blonde," and "blonde moment" get thrown around a lot. Well sorry world, we've had enough. Studies prove even bottle blondes immediately feel more glamorous and sexier once they ditched their natural hair color. Plus, gentlemen (and random hotties at your college bar) prefer blondes. Sure, the brunettes might marry them, but we get the upper hand now and that's what matters.

Not that we need proof to know that blondes are the sh*t, but science is on our side, too:

<u>1. We're better in bed.</u>

Think of some of the most iconic bombshells of all time: Marilyn Monroe, Brigitte Bardot, Grace Kelly -- all blonde. It's not all in my head, either: Studies show over 36 percent of men prefer flaxen-haired beauties in bed, while only 31 percent are all about girls with dark hair.

<u>2. We look younger.</u>

This can be both a pro and a con. You'll always be able to whittle away a few years from our guesstimated age when we get older, but it sucked being underage and carded at virtually every bar we went to. Crazy as it seems, in the caveman days, blondes were seen as more likely to be healthier and live longer.

If you want to get technical, it has something to do with the loss of pigmentation, which allows for deeper penetration of ultraviolet light that's needed to synthesize vitamins. in layman's terms, we're going to look 23 until we're 45.

<u>3. We're more feminine.</u>

No, that doesn't mean we're all super obsessed with fashion and "loooooove" shopping — rather, it's all in our DNA. Caucasian blondes — at least, the ones that were born blonde and not the ones that have a love affair with bleach — have slightly higher estrogen levels than brunettes, so they are more likely to exhibit more feminine facial features, like a small button nose, pointed chin, silky skin and way less body hair.

<u>4. Other chicks are just jealous of us.</u>

Sorry, brunettes and redheads — there's a reason blondes are seen as the more approachable hair color. In our cavewoman days, we had to fight over the attentions of men because so many of them died while out protecting our tribe and hunting for food. Paleolithic hunters preferred blondes because they stood out from their brunette rivals and were seen as healthier. That's all the evidence I need to prove guys still think like cavemen.

<u>5. We make more tips.</u>

Brunettes might be perceived as the more intelligent hair color, but blondes still make serious bank. According to a 2009 survey by Cornell University, blonde waitresses earned significantly higher tips than other hair colors -- despite their reported levels of hotness. That's not all. Bottle blondes are shown as more likely to put their foot down in unfair situations, like when they feel they deserve a pay raise. Dumb blonde? You wish.

<u>6. We're way more outgoing.</u>

Take a mental note and look around next time you're having a girls' night out. Who's the chick dancing on the table? What about the girl that always signs up first for karaoke? Chances are, it's the girl with the light locks. Besides that, we're seen as more approachable. There are countless essays on brunettes turned bottle blondes, and how they noticed more people come up to them and introduce themselves once they switched over. It's a blonde thing, and there's nothing wrong with that.

<u>7. We are spontaneous.</u>

Studies show brunettes are seen as both more sensible and more rational. Sure, they make better wives, but we have fun in the moment. Knowing how to let loose and have fun is just as important as knowing how to settle down. No need to hate on how chill we are — we just know when it's time to have a good time!"

Since I've offered you the words of a defensive, self- loving blonde, I feel it's only fair to investigate what a dark- haired maiden might have to say on the matter, as an opposing view. Here's research conducted by four unified brunettes who felt determined to resolve the question once and for all in a piece posted at, www.buzzfeed.com/sarahburton/we-found-out-if-blondes-really-have-more-fun. What they have to say is that although scientist cannot submit that the cliche' is true, these ladies highly enjoyed their time posing as blondes for this experiment. Here is the actual research they conducted;

"It's a truth near-universally acknowledged that blondes have more fun. So we, a group of non-blondes, set out on a highly scientific experiment to determine whether or not this was an actual truth, or just something blonde people say to make us feel inferior.

"After reviewing the notes in our Lisa Frank binders from fourth-grade science class, we bought a trifold board and began outlining what we would need to answer the question. In order for our data to have any weight, the experiment must be repeatable. We repeated it four times — with the naturally dark-haired Jessica, Christina, Dria, and Sarah. If it's on T-shirts and memes, it must be true, right? They say blondes have more fun. But who dafuq is "they"?

"They is Clairol — in the 1950s and '60s, ads for Lady Clairol asked "Is it true blondes have more fun?" So, maybe we got obsessed with being blondes because we are mindless sheep being brainwashed by our cattle driver, Clairol. OR maybe we are sheep that really do have more fun being blonde? Bah, bah, black sheep, you know?

"The concept was also made popular in film. 20th Century Fox. Since Marilyn Monroe first told us that Gentlemen Prefer Blondes, your darker-haired counterparts have wondered if it's actually better on the fairer side. This film is based on a play, based on a book that came out in 1925, meaning that even your grandma grew up hearing about how fabulous it was to be blonde.

"Feeling confident about our hypothesis, we gathered four blonde wigs and embarked on our ethnographic study. Science requires math, so our blonde and non-blonde experiences were compared on a five-point scale.

Test Subject 1: Jessica

My typical non-blonde weekend:

My weekends go one of two ways. I either have a crazy weekend where I try to fit in hangouts with all my friends and boyfriend, and go out as much as possible, or I stay in, relax, and do nothing but Netflix and chill. When I actually go out, I am a very friendly person, and I try to meet as many people as possible, especially if I'm drinking. I am one of those people who will add everyone around me on Facebook and then forget who they were the next morning (I'm sorry, I can't help it). One thing I must say, though, is that I don't like being the center of attention, so I was really nervous about wearing a blonde wig because I didn't want to stand out more than usual. Fun Rating: 3.5 out of 5 on my chill weekends, 5 out of 5 whenever I go out with my friends.

My weekend as a blonde:

For this experiment I decided to go to one of my best friend's DJing gigs in Alphabet City, New York. I figured if I was going to try to stand out, a place filled with people dancing would be a good place to really test out how "blonde me" would act out. And, to my surprise, nothing really changed, and I acted the same way I usually do, only with the pain of having to wear a ridiculous-looking wig on my head. My wig was pretty low quality, so I paired it with a fitted cap so it would look more realistic. Even though my experience overall didn't change, my friends and different people I met told me I looked like an animé character as a blonde.

Throughout the night I tried being a bit louder and more "fun," but then I realized that if I had to purposely push myself to be even more outgoing, then I was forcing the experiment to go a certain way instead of just letting it be. So then I decided to just have a good time and see if people treated me differently, but they really didn't! Since it was easy to figure out I was wearing a wig, at one point one of my best friends borrowed it. That was the only out of the ordinary thing that happened, because at that point I just had the little sock thing you use under the wig on. Other than that, being a blonde wasn't a life-changing event for me. Fun Rating: 5 out of 5 for sure, but I was also trying to have a good time on purpose.

My typical non-blonde weekend:

I usually go out dancing at least one night every week. My current hair is a purple-yellow mullet, which makes for some crazy freakish dancing. I have a lot of fun, but I usually don't flirt-dance, something that requires eyelash-batting at leery men. Then, after one night of expending all my energy, I stay home and eat croissants from my local coffee shop. Sometimes I do laundry. Most of the time I sit at home thinking about chores I should complete.

My weekend as a blonde:

First, I went shopping because I hate shopping, and, using Cher from Clueless as an example, blondes love shopping. There were two things that resulted from this blonde excursion: I gravitated toward clothing that I'd never wear as a non-blonde, and clothes that I would usually try on looked awful on me as a blonde (see Coachella-like shirt vs. cotton sack). I spent about 40 minutes in the dressing room, shamelessly taking selfies after every outfit change. When I finally came out, there were about 10 people waiting in line, glaring at me. I felt exposed: a pure charlatan! And to top that off, my wig got caught on the ends of the unwanted clothes rack. I pitifully pulled the synthetic strands from the hanger and cried out a weak "ahhhhh." Even though I left mortified, I spend $50: $30 more than I normally spend.

My next adventure as a blonde was to date on the Tinder. Feeling 100 times more narcissistic, I took a hilarious number of hot selfies and uploaded them to my Tinder profile. I also changed my bio to "Just a blonde tryna have fun **kiss**." While my match rate was more or less the same, messages came in more quickly and were flirty AF. I secured a date for Saturday night at a bougie nightclub and spent 50 minutes longer than usual getting ready, but my final hot, vampy goth look was worth it.

The date started out with some classic blonde fun — we danced sexily and sipped vodka like it was lemonade. Eventually, we went to a "quiet corner," and as we started making out, my wig slipped off. I couldn't stop laughing and my date seemed to like my short mullet much more. He kept complimenting it the rest of the night, and I still felt like a glamorous mermaid.

My typical non-blonde weekend:

My typical non-blonde weekend consists of running errands, doing something exercise-y, and RSVPing for parties that I may or may not actually go to. Depends on so much, you know — was I productive during daylight? Are my friends going for sure? Is there a damn train from Brooklyn to the venue that won't have me en route for longer than the actual party itself? If two of the three can't be answered with "yes," then I drink wine at my apartment and chill the fuck out. Which is very fun to me. Therefore, I give non-blonde, black-haired Dria a fun rating of 4.

My weekend as a blonde:

This weekend, I decided to do the same things, 'cause if it ain't broke, don't fix it! But I did want to see if being blonde would make it ~more~ fun. On Saturday I rode the train to a burlesque class. The day before, I had long black cornrows and met the daily minimum of three catcalls along the four-block walk from my place to the train. But today, wig, and I got no love. No whistles, whispers, compliments, or anything. Wait a minute... that might be an improvement! But alas, riding the train local from Brooklyn to Soho was decidedly as unfun as ever.

The burlesque class was a different story. The idea of being performatively sexy always scared (and attracted) me. This was something I'd been wanting to do for a while, but I was hoping that doing it while blonde would help me release my inhibitions and get into "character." And by character, I just mean a version of myself who would find looking in the mirror and playing with feather boas sultry and seductive.

I was put to the test immediately: The instructor had us sit cross-legged on yoga mats and breathe deep into our "pussies." I giggled. She gave me a stern look and said, "Pussy's how you got here; pussy's how you'll get through." That shit made a lot of sense, yo. I looked in the mirror. The blonde hair looked back and told me to get my act together. And then we (me, wig, and pussy) got into it and had a ball!

Afterward I went to a new restaurant for brunch and sat at the bar to eat. Being blond made that easier because I was like, "Damn, I might look lame because I'm eating alone, but I also definitely look fabulous." Night fell and I did that thing where I weighed my options. There were two super-cool parties I really meant to go to. But I didn't have anything to wear beyond cute hair, plus, the fucking local trains, plus I was sleepy. I called it a night early on Day 1.

Sunday:

The patron saint of being a black girl with blond hair, Beyoncé, dropped Lemonade the night before. This was a good sign! I went to the gym and watched the visual album while doing the elliptical. Gotta be honest... that shit was dark and not at the right RPMs, but me and wig had to keep running 'cause a winner don't quit on themselves. Instead of my usual one and done, I went four miles. So yes, the gym was more fun! Success.

My typical non-blonde weekend:

I'm typically out late during the week, so I like to use my weekends to relax. I typically do my laundry, walk my dog, watch TV, and then go out to a bar with friends. Overall I would say I like my non-blonde hair. I went through phases where I had bangs to hide my large forehead, or used fancy shampoo to combat greasy hair (when I learned about dry shampoo, it was a great gift). Once a year I get highlights or ombres to lighten myself up during the summer. I understand my hair is also a lot less expensive to upkeep compared to my blonde friends who regularly go in for highlights or touch-ups. Although, as I've gotten older, gray hairs have started appearing. If regularly coloring my hair to cover grays is right around the corner, why not experiment? Right? RIGHT?

My weekend as a blonde:

On Friday night, I slipped my blonde wig over my blah brunette hair and headed out to a bar to met some friends. I felt like I was playing a character, and unconsciously started leaning into it. At one point, my blonde friend Allie leaned over and asked, "Do you think blondes are dumb?" I didn't know what she meant, but then she pointed out I was giggling and twirling my hair a TON. She was right. I was... I just didn't realize I was doing it. I do think I was acting more carefree than I usually would — I wouldn't say I was trying to be "dumb," per se.

I was also feeling confident. Confident enough to charge my friend on Venmo while sitting across from her and staring her in the face. On Saturday night, I didn't want to change my regular happenings that much, so I decided to stay in and watch Beyoncé's Lemonade with my dog. What would usually be a lame night in was actually life-changing, but it's a little hard to tell if that was the wig or Beyoncé. Spending dat $$$ and hanging out with confused, real blondes.

For Sunday night, I upgraded my blond wig and went to a Game of Thrones viewing party. I was feeling very fun. But then a Tony Award nominee told me I looked bad in blonde, so that knocked me down a few pegs. With the experiment over, it was time to look at our data and draw some sweeping conclusions.

Jessica's Conclusion:

I honestly don't know why people make such a big deal about stereotyping blondes or brunettes as a certain type of person. My experience this weekend taught me that whatever perception I had about being a blonde was dumb, because it felt the same as being a brunette — especially in a place like New York City where there are so many things happening every day and there are so many people with so many different hair colors! I feel like maybe I would've gotten more attention if I had worn an orange or green wig, but even then, coloring your hair with funky colors is a huge trend right now, so maybe it wouldn't have made a difference. Overall, it was a really fun experiment to try even though nothing really changed for me.

Christina's Conclusion:

Overall, the blonde variable of my experiences led to me having more fun. But, probably that's only because I performed a role that I'm insecure about: acting sexy and immodestly egotistic. Being blonde taught me to not judge my own character. The next time anyone comments on my outrageous selfie habits, I'll tell them that it was the blonde in me. Everyone has a little blonde in them: Blonde is cool, blonde is fun, with or without the actual hair!!!!

Dria's Conclusion:

I think I actually had slightly less fun as a blonde, but this is because I'm old and washed. The blonde hair, which was very cute, did not make me want to have insane amounts of fun, nor did it inherently make fun things funner. But I think I need another weekend, maybe with longer, blonder hair, to decide!

Sarah's Conclusion:

Being blonde certainly enhanced my weekend. I think it's more about doing something different that's exciting. I bet if I were a blonde for all my life, dying my hair dark brown would be equally exciting. *Scientifically, it is not true that blondes have more fun.* But fake blondes certainly do. As evidenced by this science chart, overall blondes do have more fun.*

*Please note that the data may relate only to fake blondes or blonde wigs. There you have it. Science."

And yes, there you have it. Although it seems implausible that simply being blonde allows one to truly have more fun, judging by the fact that four brunettes got together to get this investigation underway, it may just be possible that, compared to the fairer- haired females, they actually *do* get sh*t done. (Of course, that may just be my own bias talking.) I am, however, tempted to do a little research and experimentation as a 'fake' blonde myself, just for the fun of it!

What's the "H" Stand For?!

My mother never swore around us when my siblings and I were children, but once we got older and her tongue loosened up, one of the curses I began to hear was, " Jesus H. Christ!" I always wondered what the 'H' was for and as evidenced by the results on Google, a gazillion other people have pondered the same. Unfortunately, the world- wide- web could not provide me with an actual explanation. I scrolled through multiple queries and responses to the question surrounding the subject with no definitive account for the middle initial.

What I did find was a recurring theory around the elusive background of 'H'. A lot of them seemed to dig really deep and did a bit more exploring into Christian religion and history than I was up for, but I did pinpoint one summary that works for my purposes, posted by PocketBuckle on Reddit, which reads as, 'Using the name of Jesus Christ as an oath has been common for many centuries. But the precise origins of the letter H in the expression Jesus H. Christ are obscure. While many explanations have been proposed, the most widely accepted derivation is from the divine monogram of Christian symbolism. The symbol, derived from the first three letters of the Greek name of Jesus ('Ιησοῦς), is transliterated iota-eta-sigma, which can look like IHS, IHC (with lunate sigma), JHS or JHC ("J" was historically a mere variant of "I"). For how this learned-sounding acronym could have served as the basis for vulgar slang, Smith offers the hypothesis that it was noticed by ordinary people when it was worn as a decoration on the vestments of Anglican (i.e., in America, Episcopal) clergy.[9] The "JHC" variant would particularly invite interpretation of the "H" as part of a name.'

What I guess this all adds up to is that Jesus does *not* have a middle name, least of all one beginning with an 'H', and the term, Jesus H. Christ, originally derived from an ancient, misconstrued typo! I prefer, despite this revelation, to imagine his full name as something like Jesus Horatio or Herbert Christ.

Stop Crying or I'll Give You Something to Cry About!

Did this line ever help *anyone* to stop crying? It's possible that it may have worked on some to curtail the waterworks, but all it really did was teach me to stuff those feelings way deep down so I was crying on the inside. I learned that my emotions needed to stay hidden and that expressing the 'negative' ones, like crying, reaped unwanted consequences. My Dad continually told me that I was "too damned sensitive". Whether or not I believed that to be true is irrelevant; the life lesson was embedded in me that I needed to learn how to stifle my emotions. Over time, that manifested itself as complete emotional detachment and with no conscious effort, my emotional development was cut short in adolescence. I became desensitized, keeping anyone I built a relationship with at arm's length, though not on purpose- it was simply a built- in, subconscious defense. I didn't even realize at the time that I held so much of myself back from others. I put on a good front and locked away heavy emotions like they were shameful secrets that needed to be kept under lock and key. It was as if I showed my true feelings to the world, I'd become an enigma. Unfortunately, by refusing to acknowledge things like grief, disappointment, anger and fear, I was also preventing myself from ever becoming vulnerable, which did me a great disservice. On some level, it provided me with a defense against harm, but even more- so, refusing to share the full range of my feelings kept me closed off to the rest of the world. No wonder I always felt like I didn't belong.

This is what empathy writer and researcher Dr. Brené Brown writes about in her wonderful book <u>Daring Greatly</u>:

"Vulnerability isn't good or bad. It's not what we call a dark emotion, nor is it always a light, positive experience. Vulnerability is the core of all emotions and feelings. To feel is to be vulnerable. To believe vulnerability is weakness is to believe that feeling is weakness. To foreclose on our emotional life out of a fear that the costs will be too high is to walk away from the very thing that gives purpose and meaning to living.

"Vulnerability is the birthplace of love, belonging, joy, courage, empathy, accountability, and authenticity. If we want greater clarity in our purpose or deeper and more meaningful spiritual lives, vulnerability is the path."

By the time I was in my mid- twenties, I realized I had the emotional band- with of a young teenage girl. I was fairly ineffectual at identifying or expressing how I felt. Not only that, but because speaking my mind was discouraged in my youth, I'd never learned to assert myself and struggled to form the words that would allow me to share my thoughts and opinions when they might differ from others. I was afraid to offend people with opposition and saying 'no' was hard to do. It was easier to take on more than I could handle than it was to refuse others or turn down their requests. I had no idea how to express myself at twenty-five years old. Adult conversation surrounding my personal thoughts and feelings made me squirm in my seat because it was that uncomfortable and foreign to me!

I can't, in good conscience, say that the demand to hold in my tears or face the consequences was the sole culprit for my detachment and inability to assert myself, but directives like that certainly contributed to the unconscious impulse to shut everything down inside me. It's an automatic self- defense mechanism that I seemingly yield no control over, except for the handful of times I've been able to pause in that split second when a feeling comes knocking, before it's instantly snatched away and buried deep in my subconscious. The trick to reversing that process was to be able to grab onto the emotion as it arose and prevent it from being tucked away. Practice and patience made it happen. This was a huge turning point in my life, and I know from the statements made by this author that I'm not alone in my struggle.

"Being vulnerable with myself meant connecting with the deeper, and scarier, things that were going on. It meant acknowledging my own helplessness in the face of vast forces. But it also meant being, suddenly, in a position where I could offer myself real compassion.

"This same process works in the outer world, though, too. More often than not, connecting with people through empathy actually works, and it frequently works in situations where you might think it impossible.

Empathy is the opposite. Empathetic connection implies the sentence, 'it seems like you're experiencing a lot of pain, I would like to stand by your side while you feel this way, and support you if you need it, even if I can't fix whatever is going on.' And that requires vulnerability. It does mean that, sometimes, we need to be able to connect with feelings that are dark in ourselves. It means we need to be willing to hurt just as much as someone else, and we need to be willing to do this without anything to gain."

Once in a while, something will trigger the pent up, dark feelings I have buried in the recesses of my mind. Sometimes it's those sappy, heart- wrenching, ASPCA commercials with Sarah McLachlan wailing in the background about belonging in the arms of an angel. They certainly target our consciences with sad puppy-dog eyes and three- legged cats, looking deprived and despairing! Their woeful existence gets to me, the song makes me feel sad and vulnerable, makes me grieve for others I know who are lost to this world. Other times, a ballad comes over the radio pulling at my heart- strings, reminding me of the good ol' days, when life was simple, when I was carefree and ambitious, and everyone around me was 20 years younger, our whole lives ahead of us. And then, there's a vast amount of everyday triggers; people, places and things, that drive me back to a suppressed memory that I'd rather not have awakened. The pain churns inside me like an angry beast. I may not always well up or cry in the moment, but it takes me some place else for a little while, away from my surroundings, out of myself and into the heart of the unwanted memory stirring in my head. There are certainly times when my dark thoughts provoke feelings worthy of tears, and I curse myself for not having been able to process it sooner, rather than carry all this intangible, (yet *very* heavy), baggage around with me. But it's not always an option for me to feel my feelings when disaster strikes. My role in my family is to be the calm, practical one, the worldly and unsheltered member who's seen it all and done it all and lived to tell the story. My siblings look to me for strength and support, even while I'm the youngest, and probably because I *can* react to situations rationally, rather than with a shattered heart. I'm level- headed, passive and democratic. Little do they know, I wish I could have the same emotional response that they seem to have so easily. I'm not impartial on purpose; I just don't feel the feelings I have surrounding negative situations until maybe six months later. When faced with something to cry about, I can no longer cry... I'm too damned insensitive!

How Much Does God Charge for Forgiveness?

Yes, I know, many people may find this heading offensive, but as a cynic and 'recovering Catholic', I have to touch on what I feel is the hypocrisy of this particular Christian doctrine. Apparently, as of 2007, anyway, $500 was the going rate to purchase absolution for the sin of divorce. When my oldest sister was preparing to wed her fiance', they met with a Catholic priest for Pre- Cana, which is basically marriage preparation counseling. To my sister and grandmother, it was important that the wedding take place in the church, so when the priest told the happy couple that it would cost them $500 for them to overlook the would- be groom's divorce, they put up the money. In exploring the research available to support my take on Catholicism, and any organized religion in general, I came across a piece written by Mike Sosteric that widely echoed my opinions on hypocrisy in the church. Www.theconversation.com hosts his article, <u>The Catholic Church Is A Rich Male Collective,</u> which takes a look at the misappropriation of power with- in the traditional Catholic Church. Sosteric touches on a lot of valid points that support my argument:

"Although I attended Catholic Church as a small child, I could see the hypocrisy, even as a child. I rejected that religion at an early age. Like a lot of my sociological colleagues, I heaped derision on the faithful. However, one day I decided to put aside my sociological roots and take a closer look myself.

<u>"Religion is the problem</u>

As a researcher who looks at religions, I dug around and I was surprised by what I found. The text I read showed that he (Jesus) was a leader who thought of women as equals, didn't like commercial activity, didn't think the rich could be authentic and absolutely hated the wealthy local elites. He told his students to be cautious of elites because 'they are corrupt' and lead people astray.

"He said 'they do not practice what they preach' and called them wicked, blind, self-indulgent, hypocrite fools; pretty on the outside but rotten and unclean deep within. After reading the Gospels, it seemed to me that in the story, Jesus was a charismatic and popular revolutionary who had angered local elites and was assassinated as a result.

<u>"The Big Lie</u>

The elites were afraid that should the people crown this new leader king, as they seemed ready to do, they would lose their control of power. To head off the threat, the top male elites, the 'chief priests and the Pharisees', convened their version of the Supreme Court (the Sanhedrin) and plotted an untimely death for Jesus.

"He (Jesus) told wealthy folks to redistribute their wealth and his followers did the same. Jesus and the early Christians were about equality and freedom from the 'yoke of slavery.' They dismissed political, ethnic and gender hierarchies and said we should all help the weak, not destroy them.

"In 2 Corinthians 8: 13-15, the apostle Paul admonishes the Corinthians and tells them to 'strive for equality' by redistributing their wealth. In a passage prescient of Karl Marx's famous quote: 'From each according to their abilities, to each according to their needs,' Paul reminds the Corinthians to share. 'The one who gathered much did not have too much, and the one who gathered little did not have too little.'

"All of the above was rooted in Christ and his followers' dismissal of authoritarian spirituality in favour of a radical "we are all God" cosmology. Jesus claimed to be God but "so are you," he said (John 10:24, Corinthians 6:19, Colossians 3:11).

"In other words: Don't listen to authority. Don't listen to tradition. Don't follow their rules. Give your possessions away. Help the weak. Live in peace with all people. Redistribute wealth. I am God. You are God. We are God. Why were my expectations so out of line with the actual story told in the Bible?

<u>"The Church is a rich male collective</u>

"The Catholic priests I listened to as a child didn't talk about Jesus the revolutionary; they told me the same 'big lie' the elites in the Bible told. They made me recite that same lie every Sunday. By the time I was 10, the Catholic Church had burned the lie deep into my mind.

"If you believe the Church is a continuation of Christ's teachings, this is confusing. However, once you learn the Catholic Church is a collection of elite patriarchs brought into formal power by edicts (decrees) and actions of the Roman Emperors Constantine and Theodosius, it begins to become clear. When you realize the Church is one of the richest and most powerful male collectives in the world, it comes into clear focus." Although I would've liked to see more investigation into why priests seem to have more clout that nuns, how they can invoke God's forgiveness through varied acts of contrition and why corporeal punishment was acceptable for a period of time, while the bible preaches peace among us and turning the other cheek, Sosteric exposes the fundamental contradictions that really have made me call 'bullshit' on religion as a whole. My beliefs now center around the spiritual rather than religious, and I put my faith in the abstract like karma, universal energy, the butterfly affect and everything happening according to a cosmic, divine plan. In this, my beliefs actually match up with those little discussed words of Jesus Christ, that we are *all god-* because I believe we are all connected.

Is Morbid Curiosity Just the Human Condition?

Why do commuters stop and stare, slowing traffic on their way by a car accident? Why are the hottest hit television series about death, murder and the macabre'? Zahra Barnes reports in Women's Health magazine on Dr. Matthew Goldfind, Ph.D.'s view on the subject:

"It turns out that curiosity about horrifying events is rooted in a few different instincts, all of which are profoundly human:

- While there's nothing wrong with reading up on shocking current events, a normal morbid fascination can start to spiral out of control. If you begin to feel more pleasure from the thrill of reading about tragedy than sadness for those involved, you could be desensitizing yourself to how terrible things can be.

- It's natural that when you hear of something awful happening to another person, you put yourself in his or her shoes. Imagining dealing with an unthinkably scary situation immediately compels you to figure out all of the details—so you can convince yourself that you would never end up in that situation.

- Roller coaster fans will be sure to identify with this one. When you're on an amusement park ride and plummeting toward what feels like certain death, you're in it for the thrill of being terrified—without putting yourself in the face of any real danger. Same goes for seeking out tales of death and destruction. 'These situations allow you to take powerful emotions for a safe spin and almost envision what it would be like if you were in a plane crash, car wreck, or other tragic situation—without any negative consequence," says Goldfine.

- If news stories help you feel more alert, aware of your surroundings, and more capable in case something does go wrong, that's the best outcome possible. But if you start worrying that one day you'll be the focus of your own primetime report, your morbid fascination may be taking you into anxious territory. In that case, consider sitting down with a mental health professional to figure out how to balance your desire to be cautious with the reality that it's impossible to fully live your life while always worrying about safety."

Horror movies are my absolute favorite. Every night in bed I read novels about murder mysteries or true crime. I enjoy shows like *Ridiculousness*, where they showcase people's pain and personal injury on national TV. When someone around me takes a spill, my first reaction is to laugh, and it's definitely *not* always appropriate. I'm humored and entertained by another's misfortune. Given these tendencies toward the morose, I began to wonder, ' why do I take so much satisfaction in witnessing other people's pain?' I also came up with my own answer to that question, which isn't specifically touched on in Dr. Goldfine's article. It's my personal opinion, humble though it may be, that since my life has been such a horror show itself, with extensive trauma and grief, maybe the comparison of gore and death on the big screen to the suffering in my reality makes me feel better about my position in life.

I may also have destroyed a good portion of my life in active addiction, murdering multiple opportunities that came my way and doled out pain and suffering to those around me... but, hey, at least I haven't had to saw my ankle off to escape imprisonment or offed another human or even maimed anyone with a chain saw. I (*like most others*) may have skeletons in my closet, but at least there are no bodies buried in my basement.

Who Was the Last of the Mohicans?

I can easily relay *what* was the Last of the Mohicans with the fact that it was a book published by Fenimore Cooper in 1826. Furthermore, it became a movie in 1992. In "The Last of the Mohicans", the story centers around the last members of a North American Native Indian tribe named, (you've got it), the Mohicans. The movie starred Madeleine Stowe, along with Daniel Day-Lewis, Russell Means and Eric Schweig, hunters during the French and Indian War, who begrudgingly protect the daughter of a British Army Colonel while the members of what was then viewed as an inferior race, battle to hold their lands. The imbd.com summary of the film is as follows:

"The last members of a dying Native American tribe, the Mohicans -- Uncas, his father Chingachgook, and his adopted half-white brother Hawkeye -- live in peace alongside British colonists. But when the daughters of a British colonel are kidnapped by a traitorous scout, Hawkeye and Uncas must rescue them in the crossfire of a gruesome military conflict of which they wanted no part: the French and Indian War."

There they are, the names of three of last surviving members of the Mohican tribe, the very end of the line to end in 1842 with the death of their descendant, John Uncas, according to genealogybank.com., but why was I compared, in my youth, to Uncas, Chingachgook and Hawkeye? My now 80 year- old mother, assessing me as I returned home from a typical day of outdoor play, riding bikes and climbing trees, would often characterize me as one of the last of the Mohicans. I've also heard others utter the phrase to make light of someone's dishevelled appearance. Apparently, my complete disarray, deemed unacceptable for public display, resembled Uncas, Chingachgook and Hawkeye. I was also compared to a tribunal in the 90s, after spending an hour in front of the mirror with aqua net hairspray, a teasing comb and Wet- n'- Wild make- up. The style of the nineties, big hair and bright eyes, was somehow reminiscent of the wild natives, according to Mom. Who would've thought that a tribe, thriving in the 1700s, would be responsible for a fashion frenzy some 300 years later? And it appears turquoise has yet to lose its appeal...

What DID Confucius Say?

According to my big brother, Confucius said that "he who go to bed with itchy bum, wake- up with stinky finger", BUT, I'm pretty sure that *the* Confucius, born Kong Qui, never uttered such a thing as that! However, I went to the washingtonpost.com archives to find some of the quotes that are truly attributed to the ancient (551–479 BC), wise, Chinese teacher, advisor, philosopher... This is what I found:

"By nature, men are nearly alike; it is by custom and habit that they are set apart."

"When you have faults, do not fear to abandon them."

"Chung and shu." (Chung means fidelity to one's self and to the humanity within. Shu, your connection to others. In other words, according to Confucian doctrine, if you cannot be faithful to your true self, you cannot be faithful to your fellow man.)

"It is by poetry that one's mind is aroused; it is by ceremonials that one's character is regulated; it is by music that one becomes accomplished,"

"The three essentials of good government were sufficient food, sufficient arms and the confidence of the people."

"From time immemorial, death has been the lot of us all, but a people that no longer trusts its ruler is lost indeed."

Not being satisfied with the few citations I found on this post, amongst a plethora of information about the man and his teachings themselves, I headed over to brainyquote.com to siphon a few more encouraging and inspiring quotes from Confucius' moral treasure chest. Even this lengthy list doesn't cover all of what Confucius said, but it's a decent compilation to understand the teachings and righteousness of the man:

"Our greatest glory is not in never falling, but in rising every time we fall."

"It does not matter how slowly you go as long as you do not stop."

"The will to win, the desire to succeed, the urge to reach your full potential... these are the keys that will unlock the door to personal excellence."

"He who learns but does not think, is lost! He who thinks but does not learn is in great danger."

"I hear and I forget. I see and I remember. I do and I understand."

"Life is really simple, but we insist on making it complicated."

"When it is obvious that the goals cannot be reached, don't adjust the goals, adjust the action steps."

"Everything has beauty, but not everyone sees it."

"It is easy to hate and it is difficult to love. This is how the whole scheme of things works. All good things are difficult to achieve; and bad things are very easy to get."

"To know what you know and what you do not know, that is true knowledge."

"Only the wisest and stupidest of men never change."

"Real knowledge is to know the extent of one's ignorance."

"Better a diamond with a flaw than a pebble without."

"Wherever you go, go with all your heart."

"What you do not want done to yourself, do not do to others."

"Wisdom, compassion, and courage are the three universally recognized moral qualities of men.

"By three methods we may learn wisdom: First, by reflection, which is noblest; Second, by imitation, which is easiest; and third by experience, which is the bitterest."

"Do not impose on others what you yourself do not desire."

"A superior man is modest in his speech, but exceeds in his actions."

"When anger rises, think of the consequences."

"Never give a sword to a man who can't dance."

"You cannot open a book without learning something."

"The superior man understands what is right; the inferior man understands what will sell."

"The strength of a nation derives from the integrity of the home."

"The more man meditates upon good thoughts, the better will be his world and the world at large."

"If I am walking with two other men, each of them will serve as my teacher. I will pick out the good points of the one and imitate them, and the bad points of the other and correct them in myself."

"In a country well governed, poverty is something to be ashamed of. In a country badly governed, wealth is something to be ashamed of."

"If you think in terms of a year, plant a seed; if in terms of ten years, plant trees; if in terms of 100 years, teach the people."

"Never contract friendship with a man that is not better than thyself."

"I hear, I know. I see, I remember. I do, I understand."

"To see the right and not to do it is cowardice."

"To see what is right and not to do it is want of courage, or of principle."

"Learning without thought is labor lost; thought without learning is perilous."

Towards the end of his life, Confucius summed it all up for those who not only followed, but criticized him, in this way, '"At 15, I set my heart on learning; at 30, I firmly took my stand; at 40, I had no delusions; at 50, I knew the mandate of Heaven; at 60, my ear was attuned; at 70, I followed my heart's desire without overstepping the boundaries of right." The words are from the chief compendium of Confucius's life and teachings, the Lun-Yu, or Analects of Confucius, compiled by his disciples after his death.'

Read more at https://www.brainyquote.com/authors/confucius-quotes

Is There Really No Rest For the Wicked?

Dictionary.com states "Originating as a biblical quote, *no rest for the wicked* is a proverb that means evil-doers will face eternal punishment, popularly extended to mean that one's work never ceases." Now-a-days you might hear people using the quote when they head off to their menial, tedious jobs or even return to work following their lunch break, but the expression is as old as the good book itself!

"(It) begins as *no peace for the wicked* in a 1425 rendering of the Old Testament's Book of Isaiah 48:2: 'The Lord God said, peace is not to wicked men.' The sentiment is echoed in Isaiah 57:20, which in the King James Version reads: 'But the wicked are like the troubled sea, when it cannot rest, whose waters cast up mire and dirt.'"

The now familiar version of the saying, *no rest for the wicked,* is recorded in an ancient 1574 translation of a sermon of John Calvin. In Christian theology, the passage is interpreted as meaning that unrepentant sinners (the wicked) will meet with damnation upon death (having no peace/rest).

"The biblical passage made its way into secular metaphorical contexts by the early 1700s, taking on a humorous tone by the 1800s and conveying that work and responsibilities never cease, originally with a tongue-in-cheek implication that it's due to their sinful (lazy) ways. The saying is usually used with reference to the speaker (e.g,. I'd love to stay and chat longer, but I've got a report to finish. No rest for the wicked!). A 1933 comic strip of Little Orphan Annie, where Annie has to keep after an old miser who keeps putting off replacing a church organ, used the phrase as its title, which may have helped popularize its ironic use.

"Over time, no rest for the wicked maintained its humorous tone but contemporary uses often omit any implication that one's ongoing work is due to any faults—as if it's just the nature of being a modern worker. The saying has become common enough to feature in popular titles."

One such example is the 1988 album by metal rocker, Ozzy Osbourne, entitled, "No Rest for the Wicked".

Does Cheese Come from a Cottage?

If you're a big fan of cheese, but have a 'weak stomach' when it comes to all things unpleasant, you may not really want to know how cheese is actually made. I love cheese, especially sharp white cheddar, and not much interferes with my appetite, regardless of how foul it may be. If you choose to read on about the discovery of cheese, consider this your warning, (which you'll be disregarding if you continue with this entry). Just remember, if it turns you off all things fumage, I tried to warn you.

Firstly, this is what I found on where cottage cheese came from, on the california daily press site, "Cottage cheese is part of the family of fresh cheeses that are rindless and not intended to be ripened or aged in order to develop flavor... (It) is thought to be the first cheese made in America. For centuries, farmers in Europe made fresh farmhouse cheeses with naturally soured milk, after separating the curds from the whey. Immigrants to America brought the tradition of fresh cheesemaking with them and by the mid-1800s the term cottage cheese entered the American vocabulary." A second webpage confirms that the name did indeed originate due to its being created in a cottage. What better place to corroborate this fact than on www.cheese.com? They actually answered the outright question for me.

The National Historic Cheese Making Center has its own website where it offers, you guessed it, background information on cheese and cheese- related history. The following excerpt came from their site. "The actual time and place of the origin of cheese and cheesemaking is unknown. The practice is closely related to the domestication of milk producing animals; primarily sheep, which began 8-10,000 years ago. The art of cheesemaking is referred to in ancient Greek mythology and evidence of cheese and cheesemaking has been found on Egyptian tomb murals dating back over 4000 years. Cheese may have been discovered accidentally by the practice of storing milk in containers made from the stomachs of animals. Rennet, an enzyme found in a stomach of ruminant animals, would cause the milk to coagulate, separating into curds and whey. Another possible explanation for the discovery of cheese stemmed from the practice of salting curdled milk for preservation purposes. Still another scenario involved the addition of fruit juices to milk which would result in curdling the milk using the acid in the fruit juice."

When I was in kindergarten, forty years ago, I played Little Miss Muffet in our class play on nursery rhymes. To this day I never knew that as Miss Muffet sat eating her curds and whey, she was consuming a coagulated milk product made from the stomach enzymes of the animal that produced the milk. It just sounds so unappealing, it makes me wonder who ever got the idea that it would be something tasty to eat? Well, that scenario explains cottage cheese, but what about other cheeses? Through my research, I learned that there are maybe 1000 different kinds of cheese. I can't list a recipe for all, so for this book's purposes, I found a very basic outline for how it's made at washingtonpost.com.

"Milk contains two types of proteins: casein and whey. The reason expired milk becomes "cheesy" is that bacteria in the milk grow rapidly when it gets old. The bacteria digest the milk sugar (lactose), producing lactic acid as a result. Lactic acid causes the casein to curdle, or separate into lumps, and gives the milk a sour smell. Cheese is made the same way — by curdling milk — except the milk is curdled on purpose.

Most cheese is made in factories. After milk is poured into big vats, a "starter culture" of bacteria is added to convert the lactose into lactic acid. Then an enzyme called rennet is added to curdle the milk. In the past, rennet was obtained from the stomachs of young cows. Nowadays, cheesemakers get it from bacteria and yeast that have been genetically 'taught' to make the enzyme. Once the casein has curdled, whey protein is left behind as a thin, watery liquid. The whey is removed, salt is added, and the curds are cut into smaller pieces and heated to release more whey. The additional whey is drained off, which leaves clumps of casein. Those clumps are pressed into molds and left to age (dry) for various periods of time."

And there you have it, the disgusting process of curdling milk (which no one would ever consume on purpose) and turning it into edible cheese. But there's somewhere around 1000 types of cheese, so how are the different kinds made? That explanation came from websterauntstore.com.

"Different types of cheese are made from varying types of milk and methods, and they are used in thousands of different applications, from sophisticated charcuterie boards to simple nachos. Whether you're trying to find the best cheese for pizza or your authentic pasta dishes, it's important to understand what makes each type of cheese unique. Since types of cheeses are listed by firmness, moisture levels play an important role in the selection process. Higher moisture content results in a softer cheese, while lower moisture content that is densely packed into cheese molds results in a harder cheese. Sometimes certain cheese types are freshly made and eaten that day, other times cheeses are left to age for months - even years! The longer a cheese ages, the more complex the flavors become.

While this aging process happens, a hard coating forms around the cheese known as a rind. This rind becomes thicker as the cheese ages or is washed with brine, developing the flavor profile even further. Depending on the rind's thickness, it lends a more toasty and mushroomy flavor in comparison to the creamier inside of the paste. Types of cheeses also differ from each other based on characteristics such as which type of animal supplies the milk, and where in the world the animal roams. The natural environment creates a certain type of taste for the cheese used, which is why there's differences in styles and taste between types of Swiss cheese, types of Italian cheese, types of French cheese, and specialty cheese."

Why Does the Moon Appear During the Day?

I'm fairly certain that we all learned the reason for why we can see the moon in daylight at some point during elementary school. Seems third or fourth grade science would've covered this basic phenomenon, but I hadn't committed the fact to memory, so I'm still in the dark about it. When it's daytime and the sun is out, sometimes we can see the moon high in the sky as well, and I'm intrigued to know why this is. I found the answer at vpr.org.

"We can see the moon during the day for the same reason we see the moon at night. The surface of the moon is reflecting the sun's light into our eyes. But we don't see the moon all the time during the day, and that's because of where the moon might be in the sky.

"Sometimes to see the moon you'd have to look through the Earth and we can't do that. When we see the moon during the day it's because the moon is in the right spot in the sky and it's reflecting enough light to be as bright, or brighter, than the sky."

Even Forbes magazine has an article on their site entitled, <u>This Is Why You Can Now See The Moon During The Day,</u> written by Jamie Carter, who tells us that during the phase of the Last Quarter Moon is one of the best times to see the moon during the day. His explanation for why is a bit more involved.

"A full moon occurs when Earth is roughly between the sun and the moon. That's why the moon is 100% illuminated (Earth rarely gets exactly between the two. When it does, a lunar eclipse is the result). A full moon rises around sunset, shines all night long, and sets around sunrise the following morning. It's the only night of the month when you can watch a full moon appear on the eastern horizon in twilight, and set in twilight the following morning in the west. The following night after "full moon day", the moon rises in the east about 50 minutes after sunset and sets 50 minutes after sunrise the following morning. Cue a daytime moon.

"The morning after that, it's rising 100 minutes after sunrise, then 150 minutes... you can see how, pretty quickly, the moon pretty quickly becomes a bright morning object.

"The best times to see a daytime moon is just after a full moon, when it's big and bright and, crucially, positioned relatively low above the western horizon. However, it's there, somewhere, most days—it's just hard to see when it's not much illuminated. Plus, the slimmer the moon, the closer it is to the sun, so it gets lost in the glare. The ultimate example of that is just before and after new moon, when a 1% illuminated crescent moon is in the sky, but very close to the sun, before sunrise (before new moon) or after sunset (after new moon). It's almost impossible to see, but worth hunting for.

"The opposite applies before a full moon, when the moon is rising before dusk and is visible in the west in the afternoon and early evening before sunset. The next time that happens is between First Quarter Moon and the full 'Frosty Moon'. Moon-watchers have devised eight distinct phases for our satellite, each of which lasts for about 3.5 days:

- New (rises at sunrise, sets at sunset)
- Waxing Crescent
- First Quarter (rises at noon, sets at midnight)
- Waxing Gibbous
- Full (rises at sunset, sets at sunrise)
- Waning Gibbous
- Third Quarter (rises at midnight, sets at noon)
- Waning Crescent "

There it is, nicely laid out for any astronomy buffs. Most standard yearly calendars include a schedule for the moon phases outlined above. Locate the days where the moon will be rising and/ or setting during daylight hours. Keep your eyes to the sky to catch glimpses of the Roman goddess Luna (outside of her regularly scheduled appearances during the New, First Quarter, and Third Quarter Moons), when her image shares the sky with her mythological brother, Sol.

Does In- breeding/ Incest Really Cause Defects?

I researched this topic a lot, reading many different interesting articles on the practice of incest throughout the royal families of history. Many stories covered specific dynasties and highlighted certain effects of incest and in- breeding, while others grouped multiple ancestries together to high- light a number of recorded incidents.

One such web- site was https://culturacolectiva.com/history/crazy-diseases-caused-by-royal-inbreeding, which is where the following information came from, although I cut out the last few passages referring to political histories and only included the issues it covered. The article first draws attention to the incest depicted in Game of Thrones. The Lanister siblings, Cersie and Jamie, have had three children together as identical twin brother and sister, yet their offspring are all fair- haired, beautiful angels showing no signs of any physical or mental debilitation. Daenerys, the rightful heir to the throne, is supposedly a product of generations of incestuous coupling, yet the only consequence that seems to threaten her is the idea of turning mad (which, to the writer's credit, can be an effect of inbreeding or simple genetics relating to mental health). Although no reference is made to it, Khaleesi's loss of a child in the womb could have realistically been a side- affect of her family history of in- breeding. In reality, with these kinds of practices, culturacolectiva.com tells us that "any psychological issues tended to be accompanied by noticeable bodily deformities, all of which ultimately rendered the victim probably infertile and completely unable to function properly in day-to-day affairs." It is from this site that I retrieved the following information.

The story high- lights specific and notable cases where royalty practiced marrying with- in the family line, such as cousin to cousin, uncle to niece, aunt to uncle, and yes, even sister to brother, which is detailed further on in this reading, especially surrounding Egyptian ancestry. Otherwise known as *mandibular prognathism*, there's good reason why one particular condition is more popularly referred to as the 'Habsburg jaw'... The House of Habsburg was one of the most influential royal houses of Europe throughout history. Occupying the throne of the Holy Roman Empire, continuously, from 1438 to 1740, Habsburg also reigned over several other kingdoms and empires, including Bohemia, Hungary, Croatia, Galicia, Portugal, the Netherlands, and the Spanish Empire. But there was a slight problem; their incredible status also drove them to constant incest, as they believed marriage should occur only between people of equal ranks and prestige, and they were the only family in rule. Over the centuries, inbreeding became the norm—and the later generations paid a steep price for it. One of the most recognizable features of the descending family members was a distinct deformity, a genetic disorder, where the lower jaw outgrew the upper, resulting in an extended, protruding chin and a terrible crossbite. The feature is easy to appreciate in the family portraits.

Charles II of Spain, for example, is infamous for having one of the worst occurrences of this condition on record. His jaw was deformed to such an extent that he was utterly unable to chew, and his engorged tongue, hugely swollen and enlarged, made him drool continually. He was the result of over *two centuries* of inbreeding, and it was obvious. He also suffered from dire hallucinations and convulsions. The Spanish line of the House of Habsburg finally went extinct with the death of 'Charles the Bewitched' (so called because many at the time believed that his many ailments were caused by witchcraft or a curse), who died childless. The physician who performed Charles' autopsy wrote that his body "did not contain a single drop of blood; his heart was the size of a peppercorn; his lungs corroded; his intestines rotten and gangrenous; he had a single testicle, black as coal, and his head was full of water." By the 18th century, the (Habsburg) line had been so deteriorated that it became infertile, which marked the literal extinction of the family in 1740.

Hemophilia (or haemophilia) is a rare bleeding disorder that prevents the blood from clotting, which means that its victims are prone to bleed out. Even minor bumps might result in internal hemorrhage and death. While hemophilia isn't necessarily a direct product of inbreeding, its rampant spread is. Since different monarchies carried the gene for hemophilia, royal intermarrying basically guaranteed that it would be passed on across royal lineages throughout Europe. That's why hemophilia became known as a disease of royalty. It is said that Queen Victoria is among the political culprits for the spread of hemophilia. Though it wasn't she who popularized royal incest, she was particularly adept at securing marriages across the whole of Europe, where bloodlines shared one heritage in positions of power. Since she inherited the gene and developed the mutation herself, her hiers and intermarriage policy ensured that almost every royal corner of the Western world shared the condition. When Queen Victoria married her first cousin, who also carried the deadly gene, she unknowingly ensured that her descendants—who were numerous—suffered from hemophilia. One of her own children died from it, as did five of her grandchildren later on.

Ancient Egyptians were also famous for interbreeding. If you look at the archaeological busts, a particular feature stands out: strange-looking heads due to having deformed skulls, strangely elongated in the back. This is not a matter of artistic liberty: the actual skulls found in many of Egypt's royal tombs feature this alien-like deformity.

As per custom, Egyptian brothers and sisters married often, as well as mothers and sons, cousins and cousins, and fathers and daughters. The Ptolemaic dynasty, to which Cleopatra belonged, adopted this practice. The famous Egyptian queen probably married her own brother as a result. This rampant multi-generational inbreeding eventually produced the deformed skulls ancient Egyptian royalty is known for. Tutankhamun (or King Tut) is one of the most famous examples—in addition to a misshapen skull, he also suffered badly from a cleft palate, club feet, missing bones, and scoliosis.

Many products of incest are ultimately inviable and often lead to miscarriages or stillbirths. Incestuous relationships are therefore commonly infertile ones and dysfunctional reproductive systems are a usual result of constant inbreeding, where pregnancy cannot even occur in the first place.

Distinct deformities and diseases caused by inbreeding are cleft palate, fused limbs, scoliosis, cancer and madness. For example, Maria I of Portugal, literally known as the Mad Queen, became insane after losing two of her children, her son-in-law, and her grandson. She often suffered delusional fits and religious obsession, and constantly dressed like a little girl. All this made her dysfunctional and unable to actually rule, as she spent most of her time in seclusion. It is said her howling could be heard across the royal estate, and she completely lost her grip on reality shortly after grief took over.

Charles VI, the Mad King of France, is another famous example of realistically insane kings. When he lost his mind, he could barely understand what was going on, let alone deliberately plan to conquer people in strategic battle. At some point, his delusions were so intense that he truly believed he was made of glass and that he could break with the slightest touch.

Aristocracy wasn't the only group of people practicing inbreeding, however, and when scientists took on a study regarding the existence of incestual relationships in the 20th Century, they came back with some disturbing results. Their research, reported at https://www.nature.com/articles/d41586-019-02633-1, reveals that one in about every 3,600 people in the UK are inbred.

"Rather than relying on surveys, Loic Yengo and his colleagues at the University of Queensland in Brisbane, Australia, examined roughly 450,000 human genomes from a British biomedical database. By looking at thousands of single points in the genome, the researchers were able to identify any long stretches of DNA that were identical on both chromosomes in a pair, which are separately inherited from a person's father and mother. These stretches indicate that the parents were closely related.

The researchers found that the genomes of one in 3,652 people born in the United Kingdom between 1938 and 1967 show extreme inbreeding, with the two sets of chromosomes sharing more than 10% of their DNA. This indicates unions between full siblings, a parent and a child, a grandparent and a grandchild, or other relatives with similar degrees of relatedness.

People whose genomes showed extreme inbreeding tended to be shorter, less muscular and have weaker cognitive abilities than average."

Who can say what the results would look like for the USA or any other country, for that matter. Being of Roman descension, myself, I'm afraid to know that answer.

Did Nostradamus Really Predict Anything That's Happened?

Throughout history, it seems that man has stumbled across works of the written word and applied knowledge, along with the influences of the events around them, to interpret them. Is it even possible to take an objective point of view on historical writings without being manipulated by our own experience and take on the world? In theory, it's certainly plausible, but in reality, I'm not so sure.

Christians put their faith in the prophecies of the Bible, some of which foretold of the sufferings to come and of the life of Jesus Christ. Those who truly believe the Good Book to be the 'Word Of God' also believe in the prophecies of the dozen prophets included in it. Obviously, to attest to this faith is to accept the scripture as truth.

Likewise, our ancestors believed in idols, oracles and seers. "The oracles of Greece and the sibyls of Rome were women chosen by the gods through which divine advice would be spoken through them. Although many accounts show that their prophecies were true, this is a bit skewed. They were not infallible and many texts refused to mention the errors that the oracles and sibyls made. They were not perfect and gave false information on occasions, but they were still a central part of the Greek and Roman religions." This type of exclusion of the *failed* foretellings, with focus only on what fits, reminds me of something I heard on a police show. It's called 'confirmation bias'. Confirmation bias occurs when someone gathers only evidence which supports his or her theory, to the exclusion of other evidence, and disregards clues contrary to supporting his or her preconceived notions.

In other words, we jump to a conclusion, and only focus on the findings that substantiate our claim, regardless of data that suggests otherwise. This is a clear case of a prejudicial approach to interpreting the facts, and it describes what I feel happens with the deciphering of Nostradamus' prophecies. This bias is thrown in with questionable translation and vague accounts, yet many still believe in the validity of his fore- seeings. Of course no one can rely on my uneducated opinion alone, so here's what scholars have reported, from *www.businessinsider.com/predictions-of-nostradamus-2011-12*, regarding the famous French doctor and investigator of the heavens, who many still believe to be an oracle from the 1500s.

This prediction supposedly speaks to the death of King Henry II:

"The young lion will overcome the older one,

  On the field of combat in a single battle;

  He will pierce his eyes through a golden cage,

  Two wounds made one, then he dies a cruel death."

Henry II's death did draw some similarities. The younger competitor (young lion) struck the visor of the King's helmet (a golden cage), splintering his jousting stick and stabbing the King through the eye and the temple (pierce his eyes through a golden cage/ two wounds made one). According to the doctors' accounts, as a result, King Henry II suffered seizures and paralysis for 11 days before dying a painful death (cruel death). This prophecy could certainly pertain to Henry II's death, however, one needs to disregard #1, that the joust was held during the celebration of his daughter's engagement and not during battle, #2, that his opponent was only six years younger- not quite a spring chicken, and #3, that the splinters actually stabbed him in the throat, as well as the eye and temple. I have to admit though, the scenario was pretty close. Unfortunately, it loses a lot of validity due to it occurring in 1559, when Nostradamus didn't even commit his account to paper until 1614.

Another of Nostradamus' claims bore an eerie likeness to the *Great Fire of London* in 1666.

"The blood of the just will commit a fault at London,

Burnt through lightning of twenty threes the six:

The ancient lady will fall from her high place,

Several of the same sect will be killed."

This scripture may have lost something in translation, as in English its meaning is not so straight- forward, so many consider it to be a weak link. It names the city and quite possibly the year; enough components to apply to the devastating fire. "In regards to the date, 20 times three is 60. Add six to that, and you've got

66 (of twenty threes the six) — or the year '66. London's infamous three-day blaze began on September 2, 1666." If you accept the manipulation of the numbers as an indication of the time, and plain statement of London being the location, than this correlation becomes fairly indisputable. However, we're left to interpret the 'sect' as the 'commoners' who met their ends in the blaze, which, although not counted on the census, would've been hundreds if not thousands of civilians. The only way to define the falling of the *ancient lady* is as London itself. Lastly, to label this event as parallel to the prophecy, the fact that the fire started in a bakery and not by a lightning bolt would need to be accounted for.

Many of Nostradamus' predictions have been attributed to unforeseen disasters and wars, including the deaths of John F. and Robert Kennedy, but the case can be made to disparage their accuracy as much as it can be made to support it, if not more. For every connection made between world events or people, at least two exist to discount it.

When I think about the hype surrounding December 21, 2012 and the belief that the Mayan's fore- told the end of the world, (which obviously hasn't ended), it just reaffirms my cynical outlook on prophecies as a whole. It's B. S., right? But why do so many adhere to the supposed divinity of a select few who claim to see the future? There's got to be something behind it, and it's got nothing to do with brains or personality. Paul Boyer writes for Frontline, a program of PBS/ WGBH, about the psychology behind prophetic beliefs; "some very deep human needs... are met by the prophetic belief system. Prophetic belief gives meaning to history. It gives a sense of drama to history. It gives an order and shape to human experience. We need beginnings. We need endings. Prophetic belief provides that. It also, if you accept certain interpretations that are being presented, gives meaning and a sort of coherence to current events, world events, and what's happening technologically and politically in the world. It all fits into a kind of master plan that is unfolding..."

Boyer postulates that prophetic belief offers some a sense of security in this unstable world. It may be a comfort to believe that history's most prominent events were pre- determined and played like a movie reel inside the minds of a chosen few, but then why are they so vague and open to interpretation? Is their validity only merited when confirmation bias is applied? I admit, I actually enjoy divination through Tarot cards and other 'mystical' arts, but I'm not sure I subscribe to the fore- tellings of Nostradamus.

Why Do We Wish On a Star?

Even in middle- age, I sometimes find myself wishing upon a star when I happen to catch a glimpse of a solitary burst in the night sky. " Star light, star bright, first star I see tonight," I recite the verse... unless there's someone else around. In that case, I repeat the chant in my head and secretly hope that I've not doomed my wish by not speaking the incantation out loud. I remember the words from my childhood, and assume my mother taught them to me when I was little, as her mom had shared the rhyme with her. Now I'm curious where the idea came from that stars could grant wishes, and only if we asked nicely using the approved lingo.

Someone shared my curiosity enough to blog about it on thesimplethings.com, under the title, "Stories Behind Superstitions/ Wishing On a Star", but take note, this pertains to wishing on **shooting** stars

"It's an idea that spans cultures from all over the world. But even thinking of them as stars is wishful thinking – in fact they're meteors going out in a blaze of glory as they enter Earth's atmosphere.

In the 2nd century, Greek astronomer Ptolemy interpreted them as a sign the Gods were peering down at Earth – the stars slipped through the gap in the heavenly spheres – and therefore a good time to ask for what you most wish. It's more likely their hold comes from their rarity, making a spotter feel blessed. Be thankful you only need to make a wish upon spotting. In Chile, you're also required to pick up a stone to make your wish, while in the Philippines you have to tie a knot in your hankie before the light disappears."

That makes this practice almost twenty centuries, (actually 1900 years), old. Considering the notion has passed by word- of- mouth from generation to generation, that's a pretty impressive lifespan! But it still doesn't explain my specific question about wishing on 'the first star I see tonight'.

When did it change from shooting stars granting wishes to simply spotting the first star to appear against the dark backdrop of dusk. Maybe the magical gift of wish- granting was never meant to be attributed to the lone star. Maybe the idea accidently transitioned from a shooting star and was a mistake, a misinterpretation. That would make sense, with all the wishes that have gone unfulfilled.

As I look into it a bit more, I find numerous entries about shooting stars and few regarding wishing on the first star I see. The verse, however, is traced back to its origin and deemed an American nursery rhyme.

'The superstition of hoping for wishes granted when seeing a shooting or falling star may date back to the ancient world. Wishing on the first star seen may also predate this rhyme, which first began to be recorded in writing in late nineteenth-century America. The song and tradition seem to have reached Britain by the early twentieth century and have since spread worldwide:

"Star light, star bright,

First star I see tonight;

I wish I may, I wish I might,

Have the wish I wish tonight."

This information can be found in R. Webster, The Encyclopedia of Superstitions (Llewellyn Worldwide, 2008), p. 245.

What Is at the End of the Rainbow?

For most people, the sighting of a rainbow puts a smile on their face and lifts the spirits. Some believe its an omen of good things to come or the promise of another dynamic day in a life worth celebrating, while others simply appreciate its beauty. Along with revealing what truly is at the end of these colorful, inspiring layers of chromatism, here's *10 Myths About Rainbows*, by Melanie Radzicki McManus on science.howstuffworks.com, I summarized the main points of each item to shore up McManus' delivery:

1. "There's a Pot of Gold at the Rainbow's End"- This legend alleges that Leprechauns witnessed Vikings looting the natives of Ireland, burying their stolen booty until they took sail. Inadvertently, they'd leave some behind, which the Leprechauns would claim for themselves. After seeing how cruel the Vikings were, the little men in green suits distrusted humans and hid their new- found fortunes underground. Rainbows then appeared, and their ends pointed out these hiding places.

2. "Rainbows Form Perfect Arcs"- They're actually circles, (there is no *end*!) We only see arc because the light of the lower half is absorbed by the ground, rather than reflected. The only way to see a full rainbow is from a plane, helicopter or high upon a mountain, where you're above the horizon.

3. "Rainbows Contain Seven Colors"- There's actually over 1 million colors in a rainbow, but they can't be perceived by the human eye. We can only see those traditionally mentioned; red, orange, yellow, green, blue, indigo and violet or in some cases, indigo and violet blend together as purple.

4. "Everyone Sees the Same Rainbow"- In fact no one sees a rainbow the same as anyone else, and, even more peculiar... you see it differently with each of your eyes! The reason is simple, from any position, your view and that of another, is always focused on a different spot on the horizon.

5. "Rainbows Only Appear With Rain"- This surprised me, until I learned, the fact is; they need *moisture*, not necessarily *rain*. As long as there is water in the air, from rain, waterfalls, fog, waves, dew... fountains, and the sun (at your back) hits it at the right angle, a rainbow will form.

6. "Rainbows Only Appear During the Day"- We've been told that sunlight is required to create a rainbow, and the sun goes down at night, BUT, it does still reflect off a full or almost full moon. For this reason, rainbows may form on a damp evening. Since moonlight is so dim, we can't see color in the 'moonbow', we only see white, but photography captures the color for some reason!

7. "You Can't Create a Rainbow"- Sure you can, and may have already when you were young. If a sprinkler is on and you're facing it with the sun at your back, you may catch sight of a rainbow when the sunrays hit the spray just right. It can even be done with a flashlight if the skies are dim.

8. "You Can't Make a Rainbow Disappear"- You *can* make a rainbow disappear, but it takes a pair of polarized sunglasses. Apparently, rainbows are vertically polarized (their colors vibrate up and down), and so are those glasses. They're designed to block the glare from horizontal, flat surfaces, but if you hold them sideways, up to a rainbow, they block the light from it, making it dissipate.

9. "Rainbows Appear Equally at Any Hour"- The likelihood of a rainbow appearing depends somewhat on the season. In summertime, the sun is in a more optimal position later in the day, which is when most warm- weather showers occur, making late afternoon the most common time to spot a rainbow. In the winter months, though, these conditions tend to transpire earlier in the day.

10. "A Double Rainbow Is As Good As It Gets"- Double rainbows are definitely cool, but there are actually triple and quadruple rainbows that occur from time to time. It simply depends on how many surfaces are reflecting the sunlight at the 42° angle necessary to create a rainbow in mist.

This is not only a pretty extensive list, busting the myths about rainbows, it's also a very informative collection of facts about how rainbows are created and the different characteristics they encompass. The author's approach made the science go down a lot easier than if she'd just presented all the technical jargon in a straight- forward manner. So, to answer the original question about what one might find at the end of a rainbow, it seems to me that the only plausible answer is a non- reflective surface. Otherwise, rainbows don't end, but continue, in and endless loop, forming a complete circle.

Say What You Mean, Mean What You Say, but Don't Say it Mean

Passive aggressiveness can be as much a plague on society as the overly aggressive, insecure bitches and bastards that pollute civilization with their self- centered and misplaced hostility. At least when those animals lash out, we know where we stand, unlike entering your kitchen to find a skinned rabbit boiling on the stove with no explanation! Passive aggressive offenders hide their contempt while undermining other individuals by not performing their obligations, shirking their responsibilities, moping, or putting up a front, (and in some cases, cooking up a rodent), rather than taking a direct approach to addressing whatever issues they may be having with someone. They avoid conflict at all costs.

Healthline.com covers the passive aggressive personality in a report by the same name. In it, Janelle Martel writes that people with this trait " express their negative feelings subtly through their actions instead of handling them directly. This creates a separation between what they say and what they do." Their behaviors are that of the friend who agrees to give you a ride to an appointment, then shows up late and proceeds to give *you* attitude, but denies that anything's amiss. She may even insist that she doesn't mind at all, while her brooding says otherwise. You're left wondering why she agreed to drive you in the first place, if she was so put out by it.

"However, the person may not be aware of their passive-aggressive behavior", states Martel. "Researchers believe people who exhibit passive-aggressive behaviors begin doing so in childhood. Parenting style, family dynamics, and other childhood influences may be contributing factors. Child abuse, neglect, and harsh punishment can also cause a person to develop passive-aggressive behaviors. Substance abuse and low self-esteem are also thought to lead to this type of behavior." As an individual 'recovering' from passive aggression, I can attest to the fact that *any* of the situations mentioned by Martel would be plausible causes for developing an errant approach to denying angst in the face of others and avoiding head- on conflict. Being self- conscious, stifled, facing severe consequences for mild infractions, feeling either the target of ill- will, invisible or not having your worth validated, are all likely contributors.

Investigators, though, have found an actual correlation between the conduct and certain medical conditions. Some of those " associated with passive-aggressive behavior include:

- attention deficit hyperactivity disorder (ADHD)

- stress

- anxiety disorders

- depression

- conduct disorder

- oppositional defiant disorder

- bipolar disorder

- schizotypal personality disorder

- schizophrenia

- alcohol abuse

- cocaine withdrawal

Passive-aggressive behavior isn't a medical disorder, so a doctor can't diagnose it. However, a trained mental health professional can help you identify a behavioral problem that requires treatment. However, if the psychologist doesn't find any potential environmental triggers for your passive-aggressive behavior, they may refer you to a doctor. The behavior may be the result of an underlying health problem."

There is good news for people who believe that they are passive aggressive. It takes practice, vigilance and discipline to learn how to be assertive, but it requires a lot of courage. The person will need to find their voice and then learn how to use it. When self- esteem is an issue, learning to speak one's mind and convey what may be perceived as negativity is a difficult undertaking, so patience and tolerance will be irreplaceable tools in this undertaking.

Turning aggressive behavior around will take the same kind of restraint and a level of self- control that may feel very unfamiliar and most definitely uncomfortable. Key Sun, Ph. D., asked the question, " Why Are Some People Habitually Aggressive?", and offers a response to his query on psychologytoday.com. He began with this overview, "Interpersonal aggression may take physical, verbal, emotional, or other forms, the examples of which consist of abuse, assault, bullying, intimidation, threat, exploitation, harassment, blaming, dominance, road rage, coercion, and other types of injuries in the contexts of human interactions involving disagreement, conflict, power disparity, or non-provocation." In other words, aggressives put their anger right out on display, unlike passive aggressives, who don't sign the death threats... Dr. Sun explains, "Although some explanations for the behavior are plausible, such as aggressive instinct (Freud), frequent exposure to violence during childhood, lack of inhibitory control, and possessing the personality trait of low conditionability (inability to adopt conditioned responses), their distorted interpersonal cognition appears to serve as a better account for their inability to interact beyond their dysfunctional behavioral spectrum.

"Research with correctional populations and juvenile delinquents has shown that misperceiving others serves as the cognitive cause for interpersonal aggression (e.g., Sun, 2013, 2014). Violence-prone persons have distorted cognitions about interacting with others, with the false belief about the validity of fear-backed messages or actions for the recipients. All individuals operate at different levels (from the low to high continuum) of social cognition about interpersonal reality. Violence-prone persons are guided by their misunderstanding of what actually regulates others' behavior in interaction. Their inaccurate or distorted cognition of interpersonal reality (e.g., believing in fear and violence as the method of influencing and controlling others) represents the lowest level of the cognitive stage.

"Effective interventions for reducing interpersonal aggression involve modifying and rectifying the persons' distorted interpersonal cognitions about others and about violence. In short, identifying distorted interpersonal cognitions help us understand and reduce interpersonal aggression."

Dr. Sun packed a lot of insight into this document, unfortunately it's somewhat overwhelming with it's medical terminology and professional observations. The long and short of it seems to be that aggressive/ violent people are so because they never developed an understanding for healthy responses to feelings of anger and frustration. Non- violent behavior is foreign to them, as throughout their lives they haven't been cognizant of what is, or how to practice, acceptable behaviors surrounding those emotions. They don't know what to do with ire, except allow it to overcome them and drive their aggression. It's an instinctual reaction, the most natural way for them to behave, which is why it's so difficult for them to 'unlearn' it.

<u>Why Do People Have So Much Aggression?</u>, written by Taylor Bennett and posted on the Thriveworks website, names six different reasons as to why some people release their aggression, while others suppress it.

" **1. Instinct:** Aggression is one of our many survival instincts. According to Sigmund Freud, aggression continuously builds up until it releases as aggressive behavior, at some point or another. Some individuals can suppress this aggression and use other survival instincts instead, but others simply react and release.

2. Hormonal imbalance: A hormonal imbalance in an individual can certainly contribute to aggressive behavior. For example, high levels of testosterone contribute to high levels of aggression. This explains why males are characteristically more aggressive than females.

3. Genetics: Aggression can also be passed down genetically. Children are at a greater risk of adapting aggressive tendencies if they have a biological background for it. Time and time again, father and son both display aggressive behavior.

4. Physiological illness and temperament: Serious illness can have a major effect on an individual's mood and behavior, as the stress and other mental effects may bring about greater aggression. Additionally, one's temperament can play a role in aggression. People with bad tempers typically become aggressive more quickly than calmer individuals.

5. Social learning: Aggression can be learned. Some become more aggressive due to personal experiences or observational learning. For example, children are always looking for cues on how to act, as illustrated by the Bobo doll experiment. They learn to act aggressively when they watch someone else commit violent acts like in movies or video games.

6. Psychological frustrations: It's human nature to become frustrated when life just doesn't seem to be going so well. This frustration may involve work or love, for example, and can lead to an all-around feeling of negativity. This negativity then represents a threat, which can lead to aggression."

Bennet's stance is that the key to turning that behavior around is to decipher the underlying reason for it, and address it *with positive supports.* Like the point of view in the former article, this latter piece suggests that what influences one's aggression goes beyond the conditions of their environment... nurture versus nature. It becomes their nature due to their cognitive disabilities and repetition serves to reinforce it. Whether it's through biology, or witnessing the same type of behavior around them, and because it's unwillingly tolerated by others to an extent, the aggressor does not have the where- with- all to express his/ her anger and dark emotions productively. But deprogramming is possible. It's just not easy. Programs for anger management, cognitive- behavioral therapy, support groups and medication are available approaches to addressing aggressive behavior.

Where IS the Road Less Travelled?

Philosophically speaking, the road less travelled is meant to signify the following of one's own heart despite how unpopular that directive may be and/ or possibly, the option representing following a more difficult path in life. A wikipedia contributor explains it in this way: "Metaphorically speaking, someone who takes 'the road less traveled' is acting independently, freeing themselves from the conformity of others" (who choose to take the softer, easier path in life). However, one blogger, by the name of David Orr, describes, on theparisreview.com, a specific and literal road depicted in a 2008 New Zealand Ford vehicle commercial that is meant to signify 'the road less travelled'. There is no indication given to convey *where* this little traversed route is actually located, but we know that it *is* such road because while the drama plays out on the screen, a narrator regales its viewers with a poem by none other than the famous Robert Frost. The name of the composition recited? Frost's "The Road Not Taken". The storyline, Orr describes as such:

"A young man hiking through a forest is abruptly confronted with a fork in the path. He pauses, his hands in his pockets, and looks back and forth between his options. As he hesitates, images from possible futures flicker past: the young man wading into the ocean, hitchhiking, riding a bus, kissing a beautiful woman, working, laughing, eating, running, weeping. The series resolves at last into a view of a different young man, with his thumb out on the side of a road. As a car slows to pick him up, we realize the driver is the original man from the crossroads, only now he's accompanied by a lovely woman and a child. The man smiles slightly, as if confident in the life he's chosen and happy to lend that confidence to a fellow traveler. As the car pulls away and the screen is lit with gold—for it's a commercial we've been watching—the emblem of the Ford Motor Company briefly appears."

Orr's inspiration for the recollection is simply the irony that Frost's ode to the likelihood of a specific 'road' *not* being taken has, over the past century,, somehow transformed into the most popular and well- used poem in 20th century American history. His research has shown that, "In addition to the Ford commercial,

'The Road Not Taken' has been used in advertisements for Mentos, Nicorette, the multibillion-dollar insurance company AIG, and the job-search Web site Monster.com, which deployed the poem during Super Bowl XXXIV to great success. Its lines have been borrowed by musical performers including (among many others) Bruce Hornsby, Melissa Etheridge, George Strait, and Talib Kweli, and it's provided episode titles for more than a dozen television series, including Taxi, The Twilight Zone, and Battlestar Galactica, as well as lending its name to at least one video game, Spry Fox's Road Not Taken ('a rogue-like puzzle game about surviving life's surprises'). As one might expect, the influence of 'The Road Not Taken' is even greater on journalists and authors. Over the past thirty-five years alone, language from Frost's poem has appeared in nearly two thousand news stories worldwide, which yields a rate of more than once a week. In addition, 'The Road Not Taken' appears as a title, subtitle, or chapter heading in more than four hundred books by authors other than Robert Frost, on subjects ranging from political theory to the impending zombie apocalypse. At least one of these was a massive international best seller: M. Scott Peck's self-help book <u>The Road Less Traveled: A New Psychology of Love, Traditional Values and Spiritual Growth</u>, which was originally published in 1978 and has sold more than seven million copies in the United States and Canada."

Here is Frost's original poem:

"Two roads diverged in a yellow wood,

And sorry I could not travel both

And be one traveler, long I stood

And looked down one as far as I could

To where it bent in the undergrowth;

Then took the other, as just as fair,

And having perhaps the better claim,

Because it was grassy and wanted wear;

Though as for that the passing there

Had worn them really about the same,

And both that morning equally lay

In leaves no step had trodden black.

Oh, I kept the first for another day!

Yet knowing how way leads on to way,

I doubted if I should ever come back.

I shall be telling this with a sigh

Somewhere ages and ages hence:

Two roads diverged in a wood, and I—

I took the one less traveled by,

And that has made all the difference."

Amen to that.

Are Yawns Really Contagious?

Yes, yawns *are* contagious, according to a piece on healthline.com, entitled *Facts About Yawning* by Jennifer Purdie, but apparently, the 'why' is still up for debate. There are, however, a couple of theories behind why others yawn in response to someone else's physical reaction to boredom or need for sleep.

"Even thinking about yawning can cause you to do it. It's something everybody does, including animals, and you shouldn't try to stifle it because when you yawn, it's because your body needs it. It's one of the most contagious, uncontrollable actions a body does. One popular theory is that yawning helps your body bring in more oxygen. But this theory has been mostly debunked.

"The most scientifically backed theory about why we yawn is brain temperature regulation. A 2014 study Trusted Source published in the journal Physiology & Behavior looked at the yawning habits of 120 people and found that yawning occurred less during the winter. If the brain's temperature gets too far outside of the norm, inhaling air can help cool it down."

A chart supporting this theory provides the correlations between the different circumstances under which yawning is prompted. It suggests that we yawn when we're tired because our brain is slowing down, causing its temperature to drop. Boredom brings it on if our brain isn't feeling stimulated and starts to slow down, causing a temperature drop, and lastly, seeing someone else yawn when you're in the same environment as them, happens because we're exposed to the same temperature. Purdie includes other hypotheses about the purpose yawning serves, " Another reason you may yawn is because the body wants to wake itself up. The motion helps stretch the lungs and their tissues, and it allows the body to flex its muscles and joints. It may also force blood toward your face and brain to increase alertness."

The thing that scientists all seem to agree on is that yawns are definitely contagious. Viewing yawners on the TV, movie or computer screen will even prompt others into yawning. A separate article from webmd, *Are Yawns Really Contagious?*, shares some interesting facts on the subject. Author Robert Preidt's article reports on psychologist Meredith Williamson's interesting findings:

"'Researchers have seen that yawning may not be as contagious to people with autism or schizophrenia," Williamson said in a university news release from Texas A&M College of Medicine. "More research is being done to determine the cause of this.'

"She also noted that children under the age of 4 and older adults are less likely to yawn in response to somebody else yawning. Yawning may be an unspoken form of communication, but it's not unique to people, Williamson added. Some species of primates and canines yawn in response to each others' yawns, and dogs will even yawn after a person yawns."

I find it intriguing that yawning may be a form of communication across and between separate species. I'd still like to know, though, why is it I yawn when I'm bored? Perhaps it's the only time my mind slows down long enough to recognize my exhaustion. The one thing I've always understood about yawning is that it's a signal from my brain to my body, meant to alert me to my need to rest. And I've never been one to refuse my body the rest it needs and desires!

Do We Fight Fire with Fire?

Personally, my favorite occurence of fighting fire with fire is hearing Metallica's first song off the album 'Ride the Lightning', which happens to be 'Fight Fire with Fire'. There's one line that's a play on words from another well- known cliche, the golden rule, which states plainly what this euphemism means: 'Do unto others as they've done to you'. Rather than preaching to turn the other cheek, Metallica implores the Old Testament conviction of an eye for an eye, maybe even vamping it up to take the second eye as well.

Phrases.org.uk traced the origin of the saying back to when fire was first used to literally battle other fires. "When we 'fight fire with fire' we are likely to employ more extreme methods than we would normally do. The source of the phrase was actual fire-fighting that was taken on by US settlers in the 19th century. They attempted to guard against grass or forest fires by deliberately raising small controllable fires, which they called 'back-fires', to remove any flammable material in advance of a larger fire and so deprive it of fuel. This literal 'fighting fire with fire' was often successful, although the settlers' lack of effective fire control equipment meant that their own fires occasionally got out of control and made matters worse rather than better. One such failure was recorded in Caroline Kirkland's novel, based on her experiences of frontier Michigan in the 1840s, A New Home - Who'll Follow? Or, Glimpses of Western Life (written under the pseudonym of Mrs. Mary Clavers):

'The more experienced of the neighbours declared there was nothing now but to make a back-fire! So home-ward all ran, and set about kindling an opposing serpent which should "swallow up the rest;" but it proved too late. The flames only reached our stable and haystacks the sooner,'

The method has withstood the test of time, however, and continues to be used. Foresters now routinely create roads or unplanted areas to act as fire-breaks in woodland that is at risk of fire. Although the use of the phrase in a song was back in 1984, popular among Gen X hard- rockers, thirty- seven years hasn't extinguished it from the English dialogue when it comes to discussing payback against an enemy. When we fight fire with fire, it means it's payback time and the offending culprits best beware!

Do Elephants Ever Forget?

Apparently, from what I've learned, elephants don't only have truly remarkable memories; they're also super intelligent beings that catch on pretty quickly. Although this is one reason why they are so easy to tame, at the same time, their smarts can make training sessions kind of frustrating. Their big brains mean that they aren't always so ready to bend to the will of their human trainor. And I'm not just talking *big brains* as in a large capacity for learning... I'm talking, elephants physically have the largest brains of any animal that walks the earth. They also have three times as many neurons as humans, which not only aids them in managing their enormous body parts, but helps them to retain all kinds of information.

According to treehugger.com, matriarch elephants pass knowledge on from generation to generation. They recall other elephants they've met, as well as people, after the passage of years, remember the paths to specific feeding grounds and watering holes, as well as alternative locations, and show up at the prime time to dine on fruits just as they are ripening in certain areas. Yes, research and science tells us that an elephant doesn't forget much. One elephant park, located in Muang Chiangmai, Thailand, lists the seven behaviors that they feel display just how crazy intelligent these magnificent mammals are. Their website, https://baanchangelephantpark.com lists the following as evidence of our mammoth friends' mental capacities:

"1. THEY CAN IDENTIFY LANGUAGES.

To test this, researchers found two Kenyan men from different ethnic groups, the Maasai and the Kamba. The Maasai have a history of killing wild elephants, while the Kamba do not. The researchers recorded the two men saying, 'Look, look over there, a group of elephants is coming,' in their different languages, and played these recordings to elephant family groups at Amboseli National Park in Kenya. When the elephants heard the Maasai, they showed signs of fear, huddling together and moving away from the voice. But the same phrase spoken by a Kamba man evoked no reaction from the elephants.

2. THEY CAN USE TOOLS.

(One young elephant figured out how to prop himself up on a block to reach the fruit on a tree). Similarly, elephants have been known to use sticks to scratch themselves in areas they couldn't otherwise reach, and fashion fly swatters out of branches or grass. Others have been observed digging a hole to reach drinking water, and then plugging the hole with a ball formed from chewed bark to prevent the water from evaporating, thus saving it for later use.

3. THEY UNDERSTAND HUMAN BODY LANGUAGE.

(Researchers) tested this by pointing at food hidden in one of two identical containers, and observing which container a group of captive African elephants approached. Without any previous training, the elephants picked the correct container almost 68 percent of the time. That's only about 5 percent lower than how one-year-old human babies perform on similar tests.

4. THEY SHOW EMPATHY.

A recent study observed Asian elephants comforting one another when distressed. The elephants in the study used both physical contact and vocal sounds as forms of comfort, stroking one another with their trunks and emitting small chirps. The study concluded this behavior is 'best classified with similar consolation responses by apes, possibly based on convergent evolution of empathic capacities.'

5. THEY MOURN THEIR DEAD.

... elephants have demonstrated fascinating reactions to the deaths of their kind, often displaying what appear to humans as symptoms of grief and mourning. They caress the bones of the dead with their trunks and will stand near the body of the deceased for hours. Sometimes they even try to bury the remains. They don't behave this way toward the remains of other animals.

6. THEY MIMIC HUMAN VOICES.

An Asian elephant named Koshik baffled researchers in 2012 when they realized he could say five words in Korean. "If you consider the huge size of the elephant and the long vocal tract and other anatomic differences—for example he has a trunk instead of lips... and a huge larynx—and he is really matching the voice pitch of his trainers, this is really remarkable," said Dr. Angela Stoeger, a lead author of a study about Koshik that appeared in Current Biology.

7. THEY HAVE EXTRAORDINARY MEMORIES.

Elephants can remember routes to watering holes over incredibly long stretches of time and space. This is necessary for elephants that live in the desert where water is scarce. Research also shows that elephants often form close bonds with companions, and can recognize them even after long periods of separation. Dr. Shermin de Silva, now director of the Uda Walawe Elephant Research Project in Sri Lanka, said in 2011 that 'Elephants are able to track one another over large distances by calling to each other and using their sense of smell … Our work shows that they are able to recognize their friends and renew these bonds even after being apart for a long time.'"

Note that the above fact (Number Seven) verifies for us that elephants do, indeed, remember. I found a page on the treehugger web- site I mentioned that provides a similar scoop on elephant behavior, but includes additional facts about them that are not listed here. If you're interested in knowing more, like how they hear through their feet or the way they perform in deep waters, don't forget to take a look at https://www.treehugger.com/facts-change-way-see-elephants!

Where the Heck is East Bumf*#k?

Not surprisingly, there are many places that are referred to as East Bumfuck, or East BMFK, as well as East Butt- fuck, BTFK, or East Overshoe, and they are *all over* the internet on dictionary sites. The way I understand it, East BMFK, etcetera, is a term given for any place that's not well- known to the average person. It's an isolated land, far from the hub of the city or town. The *online slang dictionary* site lists East BMFK as, "a far away and inconvenient place, " while East BTFK is described "an isolated location; middle of nowhere". As for East Overshoe, I had to turn to a different site, wordnik.com to find this definition, "Often used to refer to a place moderately far away. It generally is used in place of a city or town name when that name is unknown or cannot be recalled; A placeholder for a fictitious municipality in sample documents or hypothetical situations." But in keeping with my routine of thorough investigation, I needed to know, is there really an East Overshoe or anywhere called Overshoe in general?

I really thought that upon searching up the *city of east overshoe,* that I would find at least one entry for it somewhere, in some state or possibly even a foreign country... but I got nothing. What I learned, though, is that an *overshoe-* is in fact- an 'over- shoe', according to multiple sites, including wikipedia. "Galoshes, also known as dickersons, gumshoes, rubbers, or **overshoes**, are a type of rubber boot that is slipped over shoes to keep them from getting muddy or wet." Not quite the feedback I was hoping for. I expected to locate at least one town or city bearing one of these names, but at least there IS an answer out there, (even if that answer is that East Bumf*ck, East Butt- f*ck and East Overshoe don't exist. If I really want the location of either of these seemingly fictitious places, I should ask my mother, as according to her, she's visited them all at some point throughout her travels!

Just How Great is the Great Wall of China?

Take a guess at how far this wall extends around the northern boundary of the Republic of China… seriously, take a stab at it. What do you think? Three miles? 30 miles? 300? The actual length is estimated at 13,000 miles, or 21,000 kilometers, depending on your unit of measurement. It began its journey to greatness some 500 years ago as a plan for a decade- long project, which wound up taking about two millennia to complete. According to John Man, author of *The Great Wall of China,* it was originally built to unite China and keep out foreign invaders. Over the years, multiple areas were shored up while other pieces crumbled to the ground and had a second impediment built atop its remains. Unfortunately, Genghis Khan overcame the wall by marching his army around one of its battlements and into the country. Man presents ten facts about the Great Wall, debunking some of the myths, which can be found on historyextra.com. Some of his statements are: that "it cannot be seen from the Moon, the Chinese don't call the Wall 'the Great Wall', (they call it Long Cities or Long Walls, as it is a culmination of many walls built in each city), the existing structure was built no earlier than the 1500s, sections of the Great Wall owe their longevity to a rather unusual mortar – glutinous rice flour, there is much more to the Wall than walls or banks: fortresses, barracks, guard-towers and beacon-towers stalk the main lines of the Wall, the Wall does not contain corpses, parts of the Ming wall, notably the ridge that runs over the peaks of Simatai, are only wide enough for a single person," and last but not least, the remaining tidbit pertaining to what makes The Wall so great… "Marco Polo must have crossed it several times on his journeys from Beijing to Kublai Khan's palace in Xanadu (Shangdu)."

Ridiculous Laws Still on the Books

The details are a bit fuzzy, but I remember hearing about some law forbidding hanging clothes out on the line to dry after a certain time of day, or possibly not at all on Sundays. I didn't read the mandate on it myself, but it alerted me to the fact that there were certain outrageous and outdated ordinances still 'on the books' that I was curious to look into. I found an entire listing of such outdated decrees on the site, https://www.mentalfloss.com/article/50041/50-weird-laws-still-books. It's a compilation of bizarre regulations, most of which still exist, yet are no longer enforced, but others that, while odd, are only a few years old and need to be taken seriously. Number one, is such an enigma, which just passed in 2009! If you're interested in knowing more details regarding the laws listed below, go to the web- site noted above. As crazy as some of these may sound, take note to cover your ass, or you may find yourself taken away in handcuffs!

"1. VERMONT BANNED THE BANNING OF CLOTHESLINES. Apparently officials didn't want anyone taking it upon themselves to deny others the right to hang- dry their laundry!

2. YOU CAN'T THROW ROCKS AT TRAINS IN WISCONSIN. Seems there must have been a numerous amount of folks slinging stones at passing trains, requiring a law specifically forbidding it.

3. YOU CAN'T MAKE FAKE DRUGS IN ARIZONA. Only the *real* drugs, so get those chemical compounds right.

4. BLASPHEMY IS STILL ILLEGAL IN MICHIGAN. Keep those 'Oh my Gods' and 'Jesus Christ's' to yourself!

5. DOGS CAN'T HUNT BIG GAME MAMMALS IN CALIFORNIA. Time to train some cats to sniff out the bears.

6. DON'T BITE WHILE BOXING IN UTAH. Mike Tyson's actions in Nevada may have prompted this one.

7. SWEARING AT SPORTS EVENTS IS ILLEGAL IN MASSACHUSETTS. You're kidding- swearing is ALL they do!

8. YOU CAN'T USE A FALSE NAME AT A HOTEL IN NEW HAMPSHIRE. I'd think this one would be a given in any state, wouldn't you?

9. PRETENDING TO BE A RELIGIOUS FIGURE IS ILLEGAL IN ALABAMA. I think this law needs to be picked up by *all* the states hosting televangelists, but Alabama should really focus on the laws surrounding sexual assault after Acton Bowen's actions.

10. YOU COULDN'T THROW SNOWBALLS IN SEVERANCE, COLORADO UNTIL 2019. I can't imagine the amount of juvenile delinquents that disobeyed this law!

11. YOU HAVE TO BELIEVE IN SOMETHING IN ORDER TO HOLD PUBLIC OFFICE IN TEXAS. Sounds right.

12. BINGO GAMES CAN'T LAST MORE THAN FIVE HOURS IN NORTH CAROLINA. Gotta keep those cotton-heads in line or they'll be pulling all- nighters at the hall.

13. YOU CAN'T SNIFF GLUE WITH THE INTENT TO GET HIGH FROM IT IN INDIANA. But if you're just trying to enjoy the magical aroma of super glue, have at it.

14. ADULTERY IS STILL A CRIME IN NEW YORK. Adultery is a crime in any state, no?

15. BITING SOMEONE'S ARM OFF IS ILLEGAL IN RHODE ISLAND. Again... a crime in any state!

16. TEACHERS CAN'T TALK TO STUDENTS ABOUT HAND-HOLDING IN TENNESSEE. Yet sex education in health class is part of the regular curriculum for junior high students all over the world.

17. YOU CAN'T SELL YOUR EYES IN TEXAS. Better come up with a new plan for monetary gain, like peddling your hair, blood, sperm and eggs... all legal to trade in for cash in the USA.

18. DANCE HALLS CAN'T BE CLOSE TO CEMETERIES IN SOUTH CAROLINA. Don't want a rukus disturbing the deceased when their trying to rest in peace!

19. THEY ALSO CAN'T BE OPEN ON SUNDAYS. That's ok, there's plenty of rug- cutting in the Baptist and Pentecostal churches on Sundays.

20. FLORIDA PASSED A LAW IN 1974 ALLOWING THE STATE TO BAN ALCOHOL SALES DURING HURRICANES. Lucky for alcoholics, the weather man gives advanced warning, providing time to stock up before it hits.

21. UTAH DOESN'T HAVE HAPPY HOUR. This may relate to the state's 62% mormon population.

22. YOU CAN'T USE X-RAYS FOR SHOE FITTINGS IN WASHINGTON. I can't imagine how this law came about!

23. YOU CAN'T WOUND A FISH WITH A FIREARM IN WYOMING... so... shoot to kill!

24. DELAWARE DOESN'T ALLOW R-RATED MOVIES AT DRIVE-INS. Are there even any drive- ins left?

25. DON'T TRY TO CORRUPT PUBLIC MORALS IN FLORIDA. You can only corrupt the morals of *private* officials in the sunshine state.

26. YOU CAN'T LIVE ON A BOAT FOR MORE THAN 30 DAYS IN GEORGIA. Because any more than that would be just plain crazy.

27. SILLY STRING HAS BEEN BANNED IN SOUTHINGTON, CONNECTICUT SINCE 1996… It does make a mess.

28. HITTING A VENDING MACHINE IS A NO-NO IN DERBY, KANSAS. I wonder if shaking it after it eats your money is allowed, but if we're talking the legalities of assault, it would all be a chargeable crime.

29. YOU CAN'T MAKE SOMEONE GET A MICROCHIP IN WISCONSIN. Theoretically, you could just drag that person over to Minnesota, Michigan or Illinois to chip them against their will.

30. BILLBOARDS ARE ILLEGAL IN HAWAII. They don't want to muck- up the beautiful scenery.

31. YOU'VE GOTTA KEEP YOUR HYPNOTIZING INDOORS IN EVERETT, WASHINGTON. It could really confuse the wildlife to start taking that stuff outdoors!

32. AVOID HUNTING IN CEMETERIES IN ENFIELD, NEW HAMPSHIRE. Seriously, that's like shooting fish in a barrel. Where's the challenge in that?

33. PEOPLE WITH SEXUALLY TRANSMITTED DISEASES CAN'T GET MARRIED IN NEBRASKA. The work- around for that one has been to catch an STD after your married, you know, from having an affair.

34. EVERY TANNING BED IN IOWA NEEDS A WARNING SIGN. Following Dunkin' Donuts lead, don't omit the obvious, because there's always some ass willing to disregard common sense, then sue for it.

35. DOORS TO PUBLIC BUILDINGS IN FLORIDA MUST OPEN OUTWARD. Because inward is just plain silly.

36. RENO, NEVADA, DOESN'T ALLOW PEOPLE TO LIE DOWN ON SIDEWALKS. Reserve that for the middle of the street.

37. YOU CAN BE FINED FOR LEAVING YOUR CAR DOOR OPEN TOO LONG IN OREGON. That 'dinging' noise does get pretty unbearable after a while.

38. YOU ALSO CAN'T THROW YOUR URINE OUT OF YOUR CAR THERE. *Pouring* it out makes more sense.

39. IT'S ILLEGAL TO PLAY DOMINOES IN ALABAMA ON A SUNDAY. It's the day of rest, and domino games are way too physically straining.

40. DO NOT MOLEST BUTTERFLIES IN PACIFIC GROVE, CALIFORNIA. I can't even...

41. EMERGENCY MEDICAL TECHNICIANS AREN'T ALLOWED TO HELP DOGS IN MASSACHUSETTS. Yet it is legal for veterinarians to perform emergency surgery on people.

42. YOU CAN'T SELL DOG HAIR IN DELAWARE. I don't even want to know what spurred this on.

43. FARMERS CAN'T SELL PICKLES TO CUSTOMERS AT FARMERS' MARKETS IN CONNECTICUT. Anything considered 'home canned' doesn't meet state regulations for resale at a farmer's market.

44. YOU CAN'T SCREECH YOUR TIRES IN DERBY, KANSAS. That's noise pollution, and reckless driving.

45. YOU CAN'T WEAR A BULLET-PROOF VEST WHILE COMMITTING A CRIME IN NEW JERSEY. Wow. Wearing 'bullet- resistant body armor' literally carries and extra charge beyond the crime you're committing while wearing it. I guess New Jersey law enforcement wants a fair shake at taking down criminals in the act.

46. IT'S ILLEGAL TO BE DRUNK ON A TRAIN IN MICHIGAN. That's just common courtesy. No one wants to deal with a drunk when stuck in an enclosed space.

Each statute on the web- site is followed by a short blurb that provides more details into the specifics of the law, other laws that are closely related, or how that mandate applies to real- life situations. It's fairly tongue- in- cheek coverage, meant to entertain and amuse the reader more than educate them on the ins- and- outs of these rare, unexpected legislation, much like I've added after each one.

There are some laws still in existence which once made sense, due to the times, but gradually became irrelevant. They are widely disregarded, yet technically still enforceable. They are such that even if one were guilty of violating the statute, no officer would attempt to press charges for fear of being laughed out of the court room or chastized by a judge who didn't appreciate having their time and tax- payers' money spent prosecuting someone for engaging in a round of dominoes on a Sunday afternoon! Legalzoom.com covers even more outrageousness with the <u>Top Craziest Laws Still on the Books</u> by Stephanie Morrow.

Since there are more truly ridiculous mandates mentioned in her post, along with her own humorous commentary, I've included a few excerpts to stretch the comedy a little further.

" Did you know it's illegal to educate dogs in Hartford Connecticut? Or fall asleep under a hair dryer in Florida? Motorists take heed: If you ever find yourself driving at night through rural parts of Pennsylvania, state law requires that you stop every mile to send up a rocket signal. It's true. And if you see a skittish team of horses coming toward you, be sure to take your car apart, piece by piece, and hide it under the nearest bushes—unless, of course, you want to be in violation of state law.

"If you are a dog owner, be sure to take care not to violate any of the numerous laws concerning your four-legged pal... In Illinois, for example, it's illegal to give lighted cigars to your pets—even if they do enjoy a good Cuban from time to time. If you happen to stay in Normal , Oklahoma, be sure to restrain yourself from teasing dogs by making ugly faces... that kind of inflammatory behavior is against the law.

... many of the antiquated statutes passed in the late 1800s and early 1900s were aimed at protecting the fairer sex from unwanted attention or less-than-flattering reputations. For example, an old city ordinance in Cleveland, Ohio prohibits women from wearing patent leather shoes in public... Women in Florida can be fined for falling asleep under a dryer in a hair salon. And if you're a single thrill-seeker, head some place else. The sunshine state also prohibits unmarried women from parachuting on Sundays.

Forget about trying to publicly adjust your stockings in either Dennison Texas or Bristol Tennessee. Performing such a lewd act could land you a sentence of up to twelve months in the state penitentiary.

If you're a woman living in Michigan, you might want to check with your husband before heading to the hair stylist. According to state law, your hair belongs to your spouse and you'll need his permission before you can alter it. When visiting Charlotte, North Carolina, don't plan on packing light. According to city law, you must be swathed in at least 16 yards of fabric before stepping out into public. In the Big Apple, wearing clingy or body-hugging clothing carries a $25 dollar fine. Not all old laws aimed at women are intended to preserve their virtue, however. Pittsburgh has a special cleaning ordinance on the books that bans housewives from hiding dirt under their rugs. And in Memphis, Tennessee, women can't drive a car unless there is a man with a red flag in front of the car warning the other people on the road.

... if you want to study how public values have changed over the years, there is no better place to start than with your state and local statutes. Not only will you glean some insight into our past prejudices, but also our best intentions. "

A number of laws have to do with honoring the Sabbath, as well, and ban numerous activities from being performed on Sundays. It goes beyond forfeiting board games for the day, showing the church's influence in political matters. Shouldn't there be a law to separate church and state? Maybe there is...

The End!

Enjoy the following excerpts from "Just Kidding: A Collection of Idioms, Euphemisms and Common Expressions", another C. T. Woodburn publication available at amazon.com in June, 2021.

Knocked- up*

According to the Random House Historical Dictionary of American Slang, the phrase "knocked up," meaning pregnant, first appeared in print in 1830 (really?!). An 1860 slang dictionary defines the term this way, "Knocked up... In the United States, amongst females, the phrase is equivalent to being enceinte" (which, of course, means pregnant).

The Oxford English Dictionary (OED) traces the expression back as far as 1813 and says it's of American origin. An OED citation from 1836 refers to slave women who are "knocked down by the auctioneer, and knocked up by the purchaser."

(https://www.grammarphobia.com/blog/2006/10/pregnant-or-knocked-up.html)

Knocked Up is also the title of a 2007 American romantic comedy film written, co-produced and directed by Judd Apatow, starring Seth Rogen and Katherine Heigl. Heigl gets unexpectedly 'knocked up' by Rogen, after what should've been a one- night- stand. Heigl was too drunk at the time to recognize that she was going home with the unsophisticated likes of Rogen's character, not at all her usual type. As the movie proceeds, it unravels a heart- warming tale of personal growth and change for the leading roles as they learn tolerance and compassion, and finally come to the realization that they aren't as different or incompatible as they initially believed.

** from "Just Kidding: A Collection of Idioms, Euphemisms and Common Expressions", another C. T. Woodburn publication*

*Mad as a Hatter**

Mercury used to be used in the making of hats (prior to its known disturbing effects). To summarize the post, 'Mad as a Hatter', from phrases.org, prolonged exposure to this element was known to have affected the nervous systems of hatters, or hat makers, causing them to tremble and appear insane. The felt hatters used was often treated with a mercury compound that created a toxic dust once it had dried. Unfortunately, the dangers of mercury weren't discovered until 1965, determining that it can cause "aggressiveness, mood swings, and anti-social behaviour". The consequences of hat making in the early 19th century gave rise to the term, *Mad Hatter's disease,* as well as *the hatter's shakes.*

The earliest known printed citation, as far as I could find, is from 'Blackwood's Edinburgh Magazine', January-June 1829. At the time, the link between mercury poisoning and hatters hadn't yet been established, yet the tendency toward madness of those in the field was well known. In a section of the magazine headed *Noctes Ambrocianæ. No. XL1V,* a fictional story includes a character who refers to another as 'demented', and 'mad as a hatter'.

One doctor reported on the relationship of mercury exposure to *mad hatters* on the web, at http://corrosion-doctors.org/Elements-Toxic/Mercury-mad-hatter.htm. The article explains that, " victims developed severe and uncontrollable muscular tremors and twitching limbs, called 'hatter's shakes'; other symptoms included distorted vision and confused speech. Advanced cases developed hallucinations and other psychotic symptoms. Makers of felt hats would indeed often drool, tremble, talk to themselves and have bouts of severe paranoia, for reasons that only became clear later. Both in Europe and North America they were the eccentrics and madmen of the clothing trades, which gave rise to the phrase as used today. Erratic, flamboyant behavior was one of the most evident alterations caused by mercury." (Others included dementia, psychosis, mood swings, and various neurological and psychological debilities.)

The publication also notes that Lewis Carroll had a tendency toward developing "common expressions, songs, nursery rhymes, etc., as the basis for characters in his stories." Aside from the Mad Hatter, Carroll's

"Alice in Wonderland" also features the March Hare, another persona with a proclivity towards madness. Hares, in general, aren't known for displaying crazy or mad behavior, but, during their mating season, they can become very excitable, hopping around, seeking to attract the opposite sex. Since the mating season of hares comes with the onset of Spring, in March, the phrase, *mad as a March hare* became a euphemism for any animal or human acting crazy.

** from "Just Kidding: A Collection of Idioms, Euphemisms and Common Expressions", another C. T. Woodburn publication*

Book Description on amazon.com:

What is so great about the *Great* Wall of China? What *can be* found at the end of a rainbow? Where *is* the beef?! Throughout our lives, we ponder all kinds of seemingly random subjects and become curious of what the answer is to questions that appear to have no real solution. In this book, many of those queries are answered. You will no longer be left to wonder, " Why do we wish on stars", or " Is there truly no rest for the wicked"? This book delivers, in short, responses to these questions and many others which will give you a leg - up in conversation at your next social gathering. For those whose interests lay in the musings of the human brain, this book is perfect. It's written in very plain English, as informative summaries that will entertain any one, from adolescents to senior citizens, providing brilliant fodder for the curious mind.

This is a great reference for trivia buffs, scholars and laymen who seek to uncover answers to the random musings of the mind. A plethora of uncommonly explored queries offers a solution to the general musings of the common man. Learn why we wish upon stars, how much wood a woodchuck could chuck, what is actually in a kiss... These are a few of the topics explored in "Things That Make Us Go, Hmm".

Little known facts are packed into this book, which will satisfy the most of investigative personalities. From adolescents to senior citizens, the summaries found between these covers serves up a fodder of obscure knowledge to the most inquisitive of minds.